SELL YOUR OWN HOME

A DIY Guide to FSBO

Ken Lord

I0503592

Copyright 2020

Cover by: Jihyeon Joung

ISBN: 978-1-71659-425-0

Table of Contents

Foreword: My Duty to You 1

Disclaimer 1

Introduction 3

    What's Important? 3

    A Different Model..4

    The Final Analysis 5

    A Word of Caution...6

Chapter 1 8

    Doing Research and Setting the Price 8

    Factors That Influence Real Estate 8

    Supply and Demand 10

    Proximity to Amenities..10

    It's All about Timing..11

    About Schools..13

    The Impact of Transportation Proximity 14

    You Handle all The Calls, E-mails and Showing 15

    The Assisted FSBO 16

    Summarizing the Pros and Cons..17

    Assessing Your Own Property Value 18

    Factors That Do Not Affect the Value of Real Estate 19

    Setting your price 21

    Avoiding FSBO Mistakes...22

Chapter 2 25

    Preparing Your House for Sale 25

Ken Lord

The Ideal Situation 27

Clutter!.. 29

What's Next?.. 35

The Kitchen 35

The Bathrooms 37

The Dining Room... 39

The Living Room.. 41

Bedrooms... 42

Closets and Storage 43

Storage Solutions 45

The Home Office 46

The Laundry Room.. 49

The Garage... 50

Comparative Analysis on Home Repairs.................... 54

Repairs to Furnaces, Water Heaters, and A/C Units... 54

Paint the Ceilings and Walls....................................... 54

Flooring Fixes 55

Kitchen Repairs and Improvements........................... 56

Bathrooms 56

Roof Inspections 57

Exterior 57

Replacing Older Plumbing and Wiring 57

Other Improvements and Repairs 59

Let Dead Plants Rest In Peace . . . Elsewhere 59

Paint the Front Door 59

Make the Roof "Neat" 60

Gutter Treatments 60

Patch and Paint 60

Deodorize 61

Minor Wood Surface Repairs. 61

Cosmetic Repairs 62

Staging your home for the quickest sale.................... 62

It's a Setup 64

What About A Professional Stager? 64

It's Not WYSIWYG 66

Creating a Focal Point... 71

Some Examples 71

Curb Appeal... 72

What You're Against.. 74

Common Layout Concerns 75

Conclusion 77

Chapter 3 78

Marketing and Showing Your Home 78

Marketing Strategies for a Successful Sale................ 78

Self-Marketing Tasks 80

The Costs of Self-Marketing 81

Listing with a FSBO Service.................................... 82

The Costs of FSBO Listing Services 83

It's Time to Be Creative 83

The Marketing Idea 84

Social Media and Your FSBO House 85

Online Curbside Appeal—1234Anystreet.com 86

Social Media Positioning 86

Using Social Media to Find Your Ideal Buyer 91

The Advantages of Internet Advertising 93

Social Media as Leverage for Home Presentation 93

Lawn Signs 94

Newspaper Classifieds 97

Effective Advertisements 99

Fliers 100

Some Advice about Taking Pictures 102

Some Oddities 106

The Certified House Appraisal 108

Showing Your House 112

The Open House Philosophy 112

After The Decision is Made 116

Thinking About Holding Your Open House 118

Open Houses Sell Homes 119

Preparing for Your First Open House 120

Twenty Safety Tips 121

Setting Up the Trail to Your Home 124

Prepare a Crib Sheet 127

Prepare a Teaser Sheet 128

On The Day of the Big Show 131

Questioning the Visitors 133

Follow Up 137

Chapter 4 138

Negotiating and Working With Buyers 138

Sell Your Own Home

What is this thing called Real Estate Negotiation? 138

When Negotiation Begins 138

Some Simple Rules 140

Preapproval Letters...146

What Should Be In A Purchase Contract? 148

Disclosures—the Good, the Bad, and the Ugly 150

How Much Earnest Money to Request 151

Who Should Receive The Earnest Money? 153

Refunds on Cancellation..154

Contingencies That May Affect Purchase Contracts 155

The Appraisal Contingency...155

Appraisals/Comparative Market Analysis (CMA)...............................157

The Contents of an Appraisal 158

How an Appraisal is Done..159

The Cost Approach Appraisal 160

The Comparison Approach Appraisal..160

The Appraisal Report...162

What (Ultimately) Does An Appraisal Tell You?.................................163

And Now Come(s) the Home Inspection(s)..165

The Tasks of a Home Inspector 167

What Inspections of Home Conditions May Find...............................168

Back To Negotiation 171

Have the Facts Ready 172

Anticipating The Buyer's Gambits 175

What Can You Do? 176

Chapter 5...180

Ken Lord

Reaching Agreement and Closing Your Sale 180

Do You Need A Lawyer? 180

The Closing 181

At This Point, a Review 184

Disclosure 186

The Forms, the Forms 194

Title Insurance 196

The Home Warranty 199

The Walk-through 201

Foreword: My Duty to You

Disclaimer

This will not be an easy read. It's a nonfiction based on hundreds of hours of research and experience. It is, however, a thorough look of what you may encounter and what you must accomplish should you decide to offer your property for sale on your own. Because it is so extensive, the table of contents has been prepared to be as exhaustive as possible, recognizing that should you gain one piece of information–just one—that saves you or makes you money, the effort would have been worthwhile.

When you decide to become your own realtor, you take upon yourself the need for knowledge and all the prior experience of a person who has studied the subject, gained a license, and suffered the successes and failures that make a career. You didn't go through that and perhaps it is of little interest to you now. The successful transfer, hopefully at a profit, of your property demands that you know enough to keep you out of trouble. To that end, this book has been compiled. You may find similar advice elsewhere. This is not news; it is concentration.

The author and publisher have used their best efforts in preparing this book. There are no representations or warranties about the accuracy, applicability, fitness, or completeness of the content of this book. The information contained in this book is strictly for educational purposes. Therefore, if you wish to apply ideas contained in this book, you take full responsibility for your actions.

Every effort has been made to accurately represent this product and its potential. However, there is no guarantee you will be successful when using the techniques and ideas in these materials. Examples in these materials are not to be interpreted as a promise or guarantee of anything. Self-help and improvement potential depends on the person using the product, ideas and techniques.

Your level of success in attaining the results claimed in our materials depends on the time you devote to the method, the ideas, and techniques mentioned, and your knowledge and skills. Since these factors differ by individual, we cannot guarantee your success, nor are we responsible for any of your actions.

Many things will be important in determining your results and no guarantees are made that you will achieve results similar to ours or anybody else's. No guarantees are made that you will achieve any results from our ideas and techniques in our material.

The author and publisher disclaim any warranties (expressed or implied), of merchantability or fitness for any purpose. The author and publisher will not be liable to any party for any direct, indirect, punitive, special, incidental or other consequential damages arising directly or indirectly from any use of this material, provided "as is," and without warranties.

The author and publisher do not warrant the performance, effectiveness or applicability of sites listed or linked to in this book.

All links are for information purposes and are not warranted for content, accuracy or any other implied or explicit purpose.

This book is not intended for people who deal in real estate investment. It focuses exclusively on homeowners.

As always, seek the advice of a competent professional.

Introduction

You contemplate selling your home or other piece of property. Every Saturday you look at the realty pages in the *Star* and begin to compare what you see there with your own property; then you have a stark realisation: six percent on a $300,000 home is a lot of money! If the house can be sold in a week or less, what does the seller's agent do for the money you must expend? For that matter, if there is a buyer's agent, what must that agent accomplish to share in the fee? Face it: if the property sells in two days, somebody achieved a windfall.

On the other end of the scale, what if the property doesn't sell with the confines of a calendar quarter's contract, when the seller's agent has created advertising and the seller's and buyer's agents have expended time to show the property? Nobody has received benefit, except the "looky-loos" who simply want to see what the inside of your house looks like, and ephemeral at best.

What's Important?

It has been said that there are three important things about real estate: location, location, location. That's probably more truth than fiction, but there are many other considerations, and those considerations lie with the advantages and disadvantages of using the agency system.

If you have an automobile to sell, you park it by the curb, place an ad in the classifieds, or list it on *Craigslist* or other mechanism designed to attract a potential buyer. Such a buyer makes contact, peruses the automobile, kicks the tires, takes it for a test drive, and possibly to an independent mechanic. When that process is done, negotiation ensues, an agreed-upon price is established, you get the title notarized, and the buyer must now establish registration and insurance coverage. Generally, it's a short process, at least when the buyer has connected with the seller and the product. There are no expressed or implied warrantees nor long-term component coverage. The legalities are few and the process is quickly completed.

A Different Model

That model is not what is involved with the movement of a piece of real estate. To begin with, real estate is generally an appreciable asset, assuming marketability has been correctly managed. The adage to "buy dirt; they aren't making any more" does carry weight. Now comes the legally ensnaring process of disclosures, zoning, building codes, codicils and restrictions, and a whole bunch of paperwork necessary to exercise its options. Further comes the shaping of the property of its history and its legacy and the liability for things of which the seller may not be aware—or worse, may know but wish not to broadcast.

The simplest thing for any property owner wishing to sell is to give a nonexclusive right to a realtor to set these things in motion. This person will know all the practical and legal ramifications and function at least as a paralegal until the legal requirements demand that someone dot the "I's" and cross the "T's" to ensure the ironclad nature of the transaction is done to the point of not allowing any blowback. Even then, there can be problems: ask anyone who discovers years later that the property was constructed on contaminated ground or on properties that the engineering talent would have held as valid.

No system is foolproof. Property transfers will always raise questions. Despite this, it will happen. Sellers will be looking to reap the benefit of the investments they have made to move up as their careers permit, or perhaps to scale back as the progeny have departed the nest. While people populate property, property will be in motion.

The Final Analysis

Some sellers, especially first-time sellers, may need some professional help in selling their home. They probably shouldn't go on their own. However, many people can sell properties themselves and can save much money.

The question isn't simply how to reap the greatest benefit for the least cost, but how to do that while protecting all the legal interests, covering all the contingencies, gaining access to unfamiliar processes and knowledge, and doing so in a reasonable time.

The facilities are in place to allow you to do it yourself. It's called "For Sale by Owner." The acronym is FSBO, and most people call it simply "Fizbo."

FSBO is available to you and you can save a pile of money. To do so successfully, you need to know these things. Other tasks must be done, with a rigorous schedule by which they must be accomplished. In the simplest terms, you will face these tasks:

- Making your property salable
- Gaining the knowledge you will need
- Attracting potential buyers to your property
- Determine whether you will deal with a seller's agent
- Showing your property
- Preparing the appropriate paperwork
- Consummating the sale

This book has been prepared to give you step-by-step guidance about the FSBO process. It will advise you of some things to do. It will advise you of some things you should not do. It will also advise where some trade-offs lie, where things you might be able to do for yourself could be done with greater efficiency and protection by someone whose experience can keep you from the dead ends and sand traps.

A Word of Caution

FSBO—For Sale by Owner. It has a nice ring to it, doesn't it? You get to control your own destiny. You have full autonomy. All the major decisions to be made, you'll get to make them. The greatest share of the proceeds will accrue to you. Somebody has told you of their great success in moving their property and you see no reason it should be any different for you.

The other side of the coin is this: you assume full responsibility for all the preparation, presentation, marketing, sales, follow-up, financing paperwork, and legal paperwork. Ideally, you should know all the laws in your region as they apply to your property, what must be disclosed, what liabilities you have in the transaction, and what steps must be taken to close on the sale.

Come to grips with this: you may think you can save six percent on the transaction, and yes, on a home whose price is in six figures, a lot of money! You can save that money. If you desire to avoid paying the real estate commission in your transaction, you must be prepared to be your own real estate agent. You must do every task, take every risk, arrange every inspection and assessment, contract for repairs and replacements, file the appropriate paperwork in the legal venues of your area, and coordinate all the title and activity. Because you wish to save the commission fee does not mean that the work done by the realtor on your behalf isn't done. It must be. It must be done correctly; else, your efforts can be for naught and mistakes can hurt.

A home is not a retailer's merchandise. It's the place your heart is, where you've perhaps raised a family, where you've struggled to maintain a mortgage. It's the place the joys of daily living and the aspirations of career have had their root. It may even have some somber memories for you. Giving up such a place is not easy and it is made more difficult by your lack of objectivity.

The property is not necessarily worth what you say it is. It might be worth more, and you don't know it. It might be worth less and be difficult to sell simply because you aren't free—intellectually—to compare your home to the area, and for reasons that may not be entirely clear to you. You may no longer have children; potential buyers will be interested in the local school system. You may be retired, but area employment will be important to a potential buyer. Let's be honest—whenever we are fully invested, physically and emotionally, we tend not to be realistic.

What follows is a dose of realism. You may still make the move, but at least you'll learn what's necessary. You may wish to save on using a realtor, but you must still function as a realtor—to yourself. We will share some many options. The idea is to exchange your property minimum fuss and with full protection for your efforts.

Chapter 1

Doing Research and Setting the Price

Real estate typically represents a significant portion of most homeowners' wealth. However, that home represents stability and the decision to separate from it and "cash in" on the greatest asset is difficult. Once you have decided to sell your home, many things must be considered.

When trying to sell your home you must understand what affects the real estate market and how you must gather the knowledge needed to sell your home. Let's examine the most important factors that will help successfully sell your home quickly and for the most money.

Factors That Influence Real Estate

Demographics play a major part in the valuation and movement of real estate. Age, race, gender, income, migration, population growth, and area desirability statistics weigh heavily on real estate trends. Adjustments in family size signal the variation of property size acquisitions.

Location: Where the property is has much to do with how successful you are. Proximity of shopping, good schools, available public services, or churches can add to the value.

Interest Rates affect the real estate market. Falling rates diminish the cost of a mortgage, creates a higher demand, and pushes up prices.

The Economy: people resist moving if they are unsure of having work. When the economy is sluggish, so is real estate. An economy in recession seriously affects the movement of homes. Buyers may be unable to gather sufficient front money to use the mortgage capabilities of the market then. Good times facilitate not only higher prices but also a larger pool of buyers. Bad times produce the opposite effect.

Government Policies/Subsidies widely affect property demand and prices. Tax credits, deductions, or subsidies can affect changes in supply and demand.

Taxes and home assessments affect those who wish to invest in real estate. If the area is taxed highly, many prospects will simply avoid the areas.

Your equity might signal a better time to sell then repurchase. You have price flexibility and can easily exit a mortgage.

Real Estate Parcels are Unique and Finite. Shortages in the supply of properties cannot be overcome by making more. You may be able to increase the space utilization, but the space itself cannot grow. Real estate is where it sits. You cannot move it around. It will always be influenced by local conditions.

Inventory: Simply, how many homes or other properties are for sale within the neighborhood, town, or city? Is there an oversupply? Prices will be lower; properties cannot follow demand. Is there an undersupply? Prices will be higher; properties take time to be developed. Empty properties will identify investor confidence.

Schools: You must assure you know all the positive features of the local school system if you are to present it as a benefit of your property.

A home is easily the most important and most valuable asset on the homeowner's financial statement. Establishing and maintaining its value is a predominant concern. Because the economy so often and so severely changes, the wise property owner will maintain control over anything that can devalue that asset.

Supply and Demand

According to the National Association of Realtors, more than 85% of homebuyers and sellers go online to research what's happening in real estate market in their neighborhood, town or city ... and real estate pages in local newspaper. Begin your research online for the homes for sale on your street, in your neighborhood, or in your town or city.

The first two you may probably be able to count. In the larger geographic area, the only real assessment you may be able to achieve is to look at the newspaper's real estate pages on the days they are publicized in your area. Every one of those ads is a proposal to sell. Every proposal has something of benefit to a buyer.

Analyze all the homes offered for sale comparable to yours. See how your home is different and what you can do to market your home to attract buyers to your property.

Proximity to Amenities

Again, you are reminded that how close your property is to amenities will often affect the price you may receive. The proximity to shopping, employment, entertainment (theaters, restaurants, sports venues, etc.) will have a bearing on the buyer's decision process. As people move back to the metropolitan areas, the ability to walk more and leave the automobile at home has gained value. For you, as the FSBO seller, knowing all those details will help.

All you know now is the supply available. You know nothing of the demand, except possibly an occasional news item about employment changes in the area. Demand affects the marketability of real estate.

You know nothing about the available buyers. You may recognize intuitively that there will be a "speed" of buying simply by observing which properties remain unsold—on your street, in your neighborhood, in the newspaper.

Whenever there is a *large demand* for and a *low inventory* of available homes, it's called a *Sellers' Market.* The seller can set his price and have some expectation of obtaining it. Do a comparison and price your home slightly lower than competing properties. On the opposite side of that situation, there will occasional be a *low demand* but a very *large inventory.* This is often the case where a major area employer has closed facilities and moved from the area. Not only are there more properties available quickly, there exists an increased urgency to move them because the owner needs to relocate for employment or other reasons. This is the classic *Buyers' Market,* with fewer buyers and those looking for lures and incentives. Your price must be lower and you must be prepared for a long time in the market.

It's All about Timing

We begin with an assumption: you'd like to sell at the optimum time. To some, that means when the most proceeds can be achieved. To others, it might mean when school has let out for the year. The question has validity. When is the "best" time to sell? Is there a perfect time to sell or is the question really whether you'll sell "when the stars align," when a serious customer shows up and makes an offer.

Markets fluctuate. This expands or contracts, beginning with your neighborhood and moving outward to the country, depending on various stimuli: One stimulus might be the weather. Properties sell better in the summer than in the winter. That makes them cyclical, according to season. New school classes enter in the fall and in the spring, stay for some period, and then exit. The cycle is longer, but the process is inevitable. Consider the market is a spool of thread, open at both ends. You can rightfully assume that the active seasons are spring, summer, and fall. Travel is easy; daylight is longer; comfort is higher. Since closing periods may vary from one to three months, you can pretty much plan on fall and spring activity.

School years, extreme weather, taxing cycles, changes in mortgage rates also affect buying behavior. Nevertheless, home sales happen all year. On the off-months, there are fewer listings and a smaller competition base.

Much of the attractiveness of a home is its "curb appeal." We'll concentrate on that later in the book, but it would explain the reticence of a buyer to make a move when there is a mound of snow at the side of the street. This, of course, has less concern if the home you wish to sell is a condominium, where an association maintains the grounds. At any time, should the need arise during the less-than-desirable months, you do have the facility to adjust your price to the point of making the buyer a "proposition he can't refuse."

If you're merely moving to another location in the same area, you can be less concerned with the seasonal changes of the market.

Again, you are in control. If achieving a given sale price is important and you have no time to wait, put it up for sale now. If you have maximum flexibility available, anytime is the right time. The same things mentioned before are still in play.

About Schools

As one involved in FSBO, prospects for your property that also have children will have a strong interest in the local school availabilities. For your pricing consideration, recognize that:

Homes in a good school district can command higher prices. It therefore would behoove you as the seller to have access to the school system's ratings, particularly if you're looking for the top dollar that such a location can bring. The existence of a school establishes the area as a good location, which may also interest prospects without children.

School districts temper the real estate markets. The impact of excellent schools becomes a stabilizer for property values and sale prices within that district, irrespective of the condition of the real estate market nearby. A home built in a strong school district was a safe bet for you; it will be a safe bet for your prospect, as well. Quality schools do affect property values.

The fact that it was a safe bet for you means that your property will be good for resale and not only that, the resalability of your property becomes an attractive marker for your sale now. In a changing real estate market, serious homebuyers will assess the impact of a worthy school system on a property's value.

So now the question becomes this: is the residential property value controlled by the existence and reputation of nearby schools? Yes. Here's why:

- If the school system is a public school system, and if it's a good one, it will become a natural attraction for moderately compensated families.
- If the school system is a private school system, chances are that the system was built where it is simply that the residents were more affluent.

The closer the school, the more valuable the property.

Where good schools are, there will be other neighborhood features. Jobs, shopping, and recreation will be close, building a social fabric around the school system.

Schools close to home minimize commuting and increase student safety.

However, it's not all roses. Too many schools in an area will mean an increase in traffic congestion

The Impact of Transportation Proximity

Public transportation proximity can affect home values. As movement go from suburbs back to cities, the purchase of a home with nearby access to subways, bus, and rail lines may be of interest. If such is available to the FSBO seller, it would be wise to publish that information. On average, property values within a half-mile of transportation portals perform significantly better than those that have little or no access.

Homebuyers in major metropolitan areas may not even own automobiles and have chosen a lifestyle that has placed them in congested metropolitan areas. So if the property you wish to sell has access capability, trumpet that information. Also, recognize that the closer you are to the portal the higher your price can be.

Sell Your Own Home

What if your property is not metropolitan? The same holds for access to bus or light rail services, particularly as the cost of gasoline remains high.

The selection process will depend heavily on the buyer's lifestyle. Young, urban, professionals may seek public transportation. While they may own vehicles, they may decide that parking costs make public commuting attractive. For environmentally conscious buyers, having "green" commuting alternatives may be beneficial.

Again, there are downsides of sight and sound that will affect the FSBO seller's price.

You Handle All the Calls, E-mails, and Showing

Agents book showings, answer inquiries, and respond to electronic messaging or social media. If you choose not to use an agent, that all falls on you. It's isn't difficult, but it carries its own responsibilities and frustrations. You must accept the responsibility for communication, including either taking or returning the inquiries and following up with people who inquired. It takes only one person to be a buyer—you must be able to find that person.

You are subject to the laws of supply and demand. Just because you put a sign up in the yard or an ad in the paper does not ensure you will have people view your property. Chances are that you do not have the skills and contacts to winnow your prospect base. That means you must host the tire kickers—people who simply wanted to see the inside of your home, and, of course, some who do so with the basest of intentions.

On the plus side is this—you know the property much better than any agent. The dangers will be presented later in the book.

The Assisted FSBO

All over the country, realty companies are formed to help you in your quest of your FSBO efforts. If you have considered you'd like the maximum assistance, they stand ready to guide you through the process. They will often take your photos, measurements and help you decide on a beginning price. These folks cannot sell your home. You must still field the phone calls, handle the showings, and negotiate the offers.

Often these assisted FSBO services will collaborate with a real estate brokerage that will provide a mere posting onto MLS®. This gives even more exposure for the property. However, when you go the mere posting route you should be prepared that you may pay a buyer's commission if an agent sells your home to their buyer client.

While the idea of an assisted FSBO may seem attractive, their services are composed of component add-ons. A representative comes to your home, takes pictures and measurements. They then list your home on their website—that will generate some traffic. They then will arrange with a broker for a Mere Posting. From that point, the show is yours.

What are the advantages and disadvantages? The assistance is available for a flat fee, rather than a percentage. You can still display your own signage, and finish on an FSBO website. Of course, you can finish on a broker's website for your benefit. On the other hand, most of what they can do, you can also do, even if there's a broker posting involved.

Of all the options, you'd be wise to try a Mere Posting. Remember that if you do, you may face paying a buyer's commission if somebody is working through an agent. Expect that agent to present you with a "fee agreement." You'll still save at least half the commission of a full-service real estate agent.

Summarizing the Pros and Cons

The biggest reason people do FSBO is to avoid the Realtor's commission fee. On some properties, that is a large enough incentive at least to discuss the option. As you decide to go that route, however, come to grips with this: if you don't have the time or physical stamina to do this, you'd be wise to involve others whose insight into the business is better.

The job isn't done until the paperwork is complete. There is simply much paperwork to be handled. Should you choose FSBO, the responsibility is yours.

You may be retired and have all the time necessary to establish appointments and show each prospect through your house. That, of course, means the house must be staged at 100% of neat at 100% of the time. Don't leave a coffee cup on the kitchen counter. What's that? You work outside of the home? Pause. . . .

While we know that it's your house and nobody on the planet is as familiar with it as are you, have you taken inventory of what you need to know? Can you quote your average heating cost with certainty? Do you know the precise date that major appliances were replaced? Can you provide definitive answers about the roof, or the sealing of the basement walls, or the updating of the windows? You will learn many of these answers as you proceed. Nevertheless, it's good to be prepared.

Might you be reluctant to leave your spouse alone in the home to host a viewer, not feeling safe? Some realtors feel the same way; at least they have entertained the question and taken suitable precautions.

If you do it yourself, you can save. Few of us are independently wealthy. Most of us must sell our properties for proceeds to apply to a new residence. If you're selling a house under mortgage, it's important to at least satisfy that mortgage and have enough remaining to move forward. FSBO does give you exclusive control. You get to make all the decisions without third-party pressure. You do have a fallback position if your FSBO doesn't work.

Assessing Your Own Property Value

Knowing what your property is worth is critical to achieve the highest possible sale price.

Remember, you are your own realtor. To determine property value for your home, these steps: Agree that property *value* has nothing to do with property cost and instead has more to do with property *worth*. Property value can be assessed mathematically. Property worth, like beauty, may be in the eye of the beholder.

The process of determining property value begins with a comparison of your home to all the active listings you can obtain. If you watch the newspaper, the local new outlets, or if you can use the services of a realtor who has access to the Multiple Listing Services (MLS®), that may help. Drive around and take down addresses and phone numbers. Start entering addresses into a search engine will often provide sales information.

No two properties are complete alike, but some are similar enough to allow price comparison. All the items mentioned above now come into play. Location is a prime consideration. Simply pumping money into your house cannot overcome where it is located and, as was stated before, you cannot move it. What is the condition of the house? Is there new paint? Have you updated the landscape? Is the flooring or carpeting refreshed and replaced where necessary? Often property owners will make expensive and drastic changes to a property only to recognize that they'll not be able to recover the investment. It's wise to talk with someone with appraisal insight before you make those moves.

Other things mentioned above: where the property is located and what its general area looks like. Time of the year is another consideration, as is your specific need to part with the property. If you must have a closing by a given date, that will affect the asking price. That's the worth of the property mentioned above, in this case, the worth to you.

You must also recognize that any potential buyer will be interested in what will affect the home's resale value. Since all those considerations have been dealt with above, they will not be repeated here.

Factors That Do Not Affect the Value of Real Estate

Read this sentence carefully, and perhaps twice: the price you paid for your home has no bearing on either its worth or the price you may be able to obtain upon its resale. Yes, we recognize that a home is an appreciable asset, but that assumes that the appreciation is not merely time-based, but also by property improvement. Other considerations, many based on equity: The long-term homeowner with high equity has as much right to a fair market price as the short-term property flipper. He has some easier decisions.

The truth of the matter is that it's the land that appreciates. The physical structure actually depreciates.

Since the home is the investment, the FSBO seller must have committed to maintaining the value of the depreciable asset—the house itself.

Because you bought it in a buyer's market is no guarantee that the current real estate market and local economic conditions will permit you to make the killing on the sale you had envisioned. The passage of time is not what transforms a buyer's market to a seller's market. Some things are within the control of the owner, but others are totally beyond his control.

Of course, you want a "fair price" for your property. A buyer will not pay more for one home than for another with similar features and amenities in a similar location. However, what is a fair price? That is determined by a comparative marketing analysis (CMA). The CMA is most often done by a realtor and isn't easily obtained by a FSBO seller unless he is willing to pay for the service. Some realty agencies with FSBO interests may be willing to provide some or all the service for you.

The condition of a home affects its market value. A well maintained home will sell for more than one needing updating and repair. Be careful: cost does not necessarily equal value in real estate. Repairs and improvements are different things.

However, before you charge off to make improvements to raise your property's worth, come to grips with the fact that not all improvements will do that or are some improvement at all relative to your location or market. For current information about this, enter "cost versus value improvements" into Google and do some reading.

Sell Your Own Home

Setting your price

The CMA is an evaluation of the listing and sales prices of similar houses in the same area. It differs from an appraisal, the comprehensive evaluation of a property used to qualify the home for a mortgage. It's based on an agent's knowledge of the area where a home is located. If the agent is experienced, the CMA should be close to the appraised value.

The CMA information is used to decide the price range for a home, the fair price for a property. The outcome, by the way, is *not* the market value of a property. If the price is right, the property will have reached the equilibrium where the seller and the buyer are satisfied. That way the seller doesn't lose money and the property's movement is sluggish.

If you can find an agency that works with FSBO sellers, ask for a CMA. There may be a fee, though many may provide the free analysis in anticipation of a listing. Start with those whose advertisements you see frequently. A good agent should be able to give you a rough estimate of what houses sell for per square foot in the area.

The key to the success of a CMA is its objectivity. If you tell the agent what you think the property is worth, you've biased the outcome. The CMA analyst doesn't need to know what you paid for it, what you wish to realize from its sale, what the balance on your current mortgage, or the fact that the property has been in your family for several generations. If you can obtain a CMA from more than one person, you can develop averages that may be more unbiased.

How is a CMA Prepared? Much of the information about your property is available in public records. If you have an agent who works with FSBO sellers, then the Multiple Listing System (MLS) is a great source of comparison of properties recently sold and currently for sale.

It isn't complicated. Three comparable properties within a mile should be sufficient to conduct a CMA. In a rapidly moving market, sometimes the agent will look at three that have sold recently. Properties are as identical as possible.

Use CMA listings with a view of your property. Don't overlook this, as the agent may be able to make helpful suggestions. Other sources include active listings, pending listings, and listings that have expired. Location is important, the key consideration.

These things are examined in a CMA: comparable square footage, features, age, and amenities (with upgrades).

The report of the CMA will contain a recommended selling price range, which will include the probable price under the current conditions. Properties selected may have some differences, such as age, size, condition, or architectural style.

Avoiding FSBO Mistakes

Should you try selling your home yourself? Selling a house is not easy. It takes time and work, but you can do it. Here are some points to consider:

For upscale or distant properties, hire an agent. If any savings can be achieved on these properties, you'll burn them away with the extraordinary activities the properties demand. If your property has an extraordinary price ticket, recognize that it has an exclusive clientele. Find an agent who caters to that clientele.

Sell Your Own Home

Where the FSBO strategy can work best is in the broad middle market, with the property you inhabit or which may be close by.

If you can't divorce yourself from your emotions, from memories, from where you raised your family, from all the pictures in your albums, and see the FSBO transaction objectively, you're asking for trouble.

You have some fundamental questions to answer, not the least of which is whether you really have time to do what you must do. It takes time to research your home's value. Do you have the skills to prepare marketing materials or will you have to contract that to someone else anyway? What about the time necessary to "clean up the clutter," host open houses on the weekends and showings at any time. That could take a while. Some folks will suggest you've taken on a part-time job. You can mitigate that somewhat by establishing showing days and showing hours and stick to them.

There isn't anything more difficult about this that attempting to establish a correct price. You want top dollar—that's a given. You also want to "move" the property quickly, perhaps. Somewhere in that mix is a set of tasks that will obtain the best return for your property. You can assess your own competition by visiting local open houses. If nothing else, you can't assess curb appeal on the Internet.

You can also gain a better understanding of what your home should sell for by arranging—and paying for—an appraisal. That isn't cheap, with costs averaging $400. A professional appraiser has no dog in the fight. You'll get an honest answer. For similar prices, you can obtain a home inspection. You may have to do so anyway. This will highlight the things you should change, any legally required disclosures, and any defects that may need adjustment.

It's also fair to expect a potential buyer to believe that because your house is FSBO, it'll be less expensive, and prospects might attempt to leverage that impression. Counter that with the observation that because you do more of the work, the buyer has less stress.

Chapter 2

Preparing Your House for Sale

This will be a lengthy and difficult chapter to read and digest, but what is presented here is important. If you take every tip, every practice, and every recommendation, the chances are high that you might want not to sell the place. You fell in love with the home when you first bought it. Over the years, you got used to it—and it got used to you. Correct us if we're wrong: your house no longer looks like the House Beautiful you first viewed, so many moons ago.

For some reason, you have decided to move. Now comes the tough part: letting go. This is the house where you raised your family, perhaps. The "tic" marks on the frame on the kitchen door has detailed every inch of growth.

"He" may have an outstanding woodshop in the basement and is reluctant to move the equipment. Perhaps there is an outbuilding where he kept lawn machinery, an outdoor grill, the snow blower, and snowmobile. He can't somehow come to grips with leaving that.

The backyard has a horseshoe pit, a badminton court, and an in-ground swimming pool. It's hard to leave those, particularly if you have memories of children and grandchildren anchored there.

"She" loves the kitchen that she's worked in for many years. Yes, it could be updated, but it works for her. She likes the craft room and the family room where the massive entertainment center is located. Yes, she'd like the bathrooms updated, but these have functioned for years, and, after all, this was her mother's house and that memory strain is still strong.

Beware the siren lullaby of personal comfort. You've decided to move—to a new job, to a smaller abode, to a retirement home, or to be close to your daughter. Don't let your emotions sabotage your decision.

Nevertheless, it is time for another, and most valuable, decision: to dissociate yourself with your home. Your home is merely a house—a commodity to be sold. Decide to let go and focus on the steps that lie between today and the future. As your house goes up for sale, it's time to say "Good-bye" and start getting things together to prepare the house to make it most inviting to the next owner. Talk to yourself. Tell yourself that selling your home can be stressful.

Unless you're in the business of buying "fixer-uppers," performing repairs and updates, and "flipping the property," the decision to sell your home was not an easy one, and perhaps at this point you're not truly ready. You'll find many sources of advice, but hold this one point: you should not sell until you're ready to make a transformation in your life. That decision to sell now places you in a position to undertake much work and perhaps considerable expense. If you're ready to sell your house, you must do several things to make it attractive to a buyer. We're going to focus this chapter on those.

You must stop thinking of the building in which you live as "home" and begin to think of it as an "it"—a product that you wish to bring to market. You have something to sell and if it's presented well, you'll be fortunate to see it sold. Start now with at least these resolutions:

- I will not attempt to sell my home at a price higher than the market currently will allow.

- I recognize that this house is "lived in," and I really want to see a prospective buyer look at my house as a place the buyer can place those important treasures of his or her life.

- I will take the steps necessary to make the house presentable and inviting, recognizing that it takes money to make money. If you want to sell your house "as is," that's all right too, if you're willing to give away a substantial amount of its value.

- I will be willing to make the sacrifices necessary to "tidy up" my house and my life.

- I will cherish the memories I've had in the home, but I will focus on the next step and the memories yet to be made.

The Ideal Situation

Three watchwords to Consider as you begin: 1) open, 2) breezy, and 3) minimalist.

When you bought this house, what was in it? If it were a new house, chances are that there was little, if anything in it at all. Remember. Was there a giant sofa that commanded the floor space of the living room? How did the bookshelves appear? What about windows and curtains? Were the walls covered with the memorabilia of sports victories? Were the walls garish colors or did they have painted accents? What about the floor? The appliances? And on and on.

Ideally, the house you wish to present for sale is empty, unless . . . and it's a big "unless." If you live in the house, where do you put all your junk? It's simply lying around. Nobody wants to spend any time in your junky house. The word gets around. You want the space to be open and to appear to be larger than it is. You want the airflow throughout the home to be light and breezy. You want the lighting to be extraordinary. You want the least amount of "you" in the house that you can achieve when you have it on the market.

We began this book with an assumption, recall. We assumed that FSBO was a way to save a pile of money on the sale of your home. This chapter, if you take all the suggestions, will result in your spending all that money and more. More importantly, what is contained herein will increase the value of your property—up to a point—which, in turn, will return more money. So we have a pair of intersecting curves here, and the idea is to do enough to raise that selling price somewhere close to the maximum while keeping the out-of-pocket costs somewhere near the minimum. Of course, what you do is strictly up to you. We'll show you the picture and help evaluate the options. The rest is up to you.

Here's the approach. The first thing you can do to get this property ready is to throw away—or at least stow—a bunch of stuff. Next, we'll concentrate upon the infrastructure of your home, how you should inspect it, and how—if necessary—it should be repaired. Finally, we'll talk about how your home should be presented, how it should be *staged* for viewing and subsequent sale.

You never get a second chance to make a good first impression. As you wanted it when you bought this house, prospective buyers want to see your home in "showplace" condition. Think about what attracted you to the house. You may have evaluated every number and checked many properties, but there had to be one thing that drew you to this house in particular. Theoretically, we should perhaps focus first on "curb appeal," how your house—and your property—look from the outside. Few will want to see the inside unless they are pleased with the outside. We'll talk about that presently.

As we develop the task list that is this chapter, however, you need to come to grips with this: you need resources to do these things, specifically time, then, of course, some funds. Don't think because you have decided on FSBO that the decision and a sign will move the property. Remember, that besides being your own real estate agent, you are totally responsible for all that must be done. That doesn't change because you chose to do some selling chores alone. It is realistic to plan on at least a month of full-time work to get your property ready to sell. If you're trying to do this and work a job, you either must plan on a longer preparation or prepared to be a general contractor and begin to shop out the various projects to qualified trades people.

So let's begin on the inside, with the greatest impediment to a speedy sale . . .

Clutter!

Clutter is the detritus of living. It's everything you've ever bought, refused to throw away, and either haven't found a place for it to "live," or are the beneficiary of appropriate upbringing that should have taught you that there exists "a place for everything and everything goes in its place." You may not be as bad as the hoarders you see on television, but it if you aren't willing to devalue anything, the piles will continue to grow. A good maxim to use is this: if you haven't used the item for a year or more, out it goes.

Understand this. You can do many things to your home to enhance its sale, but if you don't declutter it, that work and expense will have been for naught. A good rule of thumb is that your first "sweep" of your home should dispose of at least a third of your clutter. If you don't need it, give it away. Make a few shekels on it with a yard sale or simply give it to the Salvation Army or other charity. Six things you can do as you declutter:

- Keep it in the room
- Pack it for movement
- Pack it to sell
- Pack it to donate
- Discard it as trash
- Discard it as recyclables

While your property is up for sale, you need to scale back to the essentials. Here's how:

First, don't try to do the entire house at once. Pick a room, block off an hour, gather plastic bins of various sizes, several boxes (to be used to dispatch the clutter), and some construction-sized plastic trash bags. Now determine to use them—all of them.

Next, don't unclutter one room and merely carry the clutter to another room "for later evaluation."

Get a box and label it *Donate*. In that box will go what you can do without, either here or at your destination. Included here are those books and magazines you no longer need. Yes, you can put them in another box marked *Recycle* if you wish. Nursing homes and assisted-living facilities would relish previous issues of current magazines for their clients or books for the in-house library. Local hospitals welcome such donations.

Get two boxes and label them *Keep and Pack*. In the *Keep* box will go the things you consider essential but which you can get along without while the property is for sale. Those things will be returned to the room once you have done a thorough cleaning, and ultimately will be positioned for the big show. Remember, you have decided to sell this house. Keep this box in the room where you're working, but as you fill it, move the *Pack* box into a garage or other central point. When you have finished the room, carry the *Pack* boxes to the temporary storage site. We'll detail the kinds of things that should go, presently. Meanwhile, avoid the temptation to use your garage or family room as a storage locker. Obtain space off premises where you can put your things temporarily. Resist the temptation to have a storage contained dropped off in your driveway. The garage will be the last place you'll go to clear clutter, so it will be the transient point.

Get a box and label it *Sell*. In this box will go the things you decide to discard but are in good enough condition to move in a garage or yard sale. Over time, as you work on individual rooms, you'll develop more boxes to sell. As you complete the job, put the boxes in the garage until you have volume enough to justify a neighborhood sale. Then resolve that when you put your things out for sale—if they don't sell—they will be donated.

The strongest advice you can hear at this point is this: handle something once then decide. If you don't, you'll be picking the same item up repeatedly, unable to decide in the face of the fact that you recognize a decision is required. Generally, your approach to clutter should contain at least these steps:

You need to remove from your premises about a third of what you have, and handle it as mentioned.

Clear your bookcases. Remove all books. Put the ones you wish to keep in a box in the garage. If your shelves hold collections, pack those collections carefully, but get them from the living space. If you need to have something on those shelves, small items—statues, flowers, pictures—would be appropriate, if they are not your sales awards and the gallery of children and grandchildren. Remember, a prospective buyer wants to visualize his or her awards, knickknacks, and family pictures in that space.

Of course, you must keep some essential items. Translucent tubs or small boxes stored in cabinets and closets should be sufficient. You need to get at these things, of course, to continue living on the premises, but this is the first step of packing for the move. Remember to return them to their containers when they are used.

Recognize that decluttering is something you will do daily until you move. It's something that you'll attempt in a hurry when a prospect has requested an appointment. You would be wise to begin the process early in the morning then allow yourself some time to work on each room. Apportion that time throughout the week or two that you'll take to do the work. Do not try to do it all at once; there are detours all along the way, not the least of which is the time you sit and stare at something that has evoked a strong memory. Some folks who make decluttering a business will advise you to set a timer and to live by it. Why not make it a family activity?

Plan on each session taking about an hour. Set your timer for 45 minutes. The remaining 15 minutes can be used to remove and restore what you have extracted. Make another resolution here: when you pick something up, do something *final* with it. By "final," we mean for you to handle it—not pick it up here and set it down there. Pick it up, evaluate what you wish to do with it, decide, and then put it in the appropriate container. Don't second-guess yourself and go fish things from their box. That is self-defeating behavior. Look at it; decided what to do with it; then put it where it belongs.

Translucent tubs are great for things you wish to hang onto and use. Make certain that you label their contents. For those things that will be put in a yard sale or donated, consider Banker's Boxes. Any size cardboard box will do, of course, but the Banker's Boxes are uniform, have lids and handholds, and you won't be tempted to put too much weight into them. Reasonable-duty Banker's Boxes will run you about two dollars apiece, in quantities of ten.

There is one more box—the *Unsure*. Mark this one with a large question mark (?). Into this box will go the items on which you simply cannot make an immediate decision. Two things are important about this box: 1) it needs to be a small box; you want to put few things in it, and 2) you must resolve to decide about the items in the box within the remaining 15 minutes of the hour.

The remaining two containers are for total disposal. These are trash bags and the recycling bin. You can use the trash bags in the room itself. Sometimes putting the trash bags into a large wastebasket makes using them much easier. If you expect to recycle some items, then a separate trash bag might be useful. Here you might put your bottles and cans on which you can receive the return of deposit into something you can carry to the recycle center. Other items that must be recycled where you live, such as cardboard, tin, or glass should be separated for inclusion in the municipal container, as required.

When the Session is Complete

At this point, there may be panic. Before you began this process, there was at least some semblance of neatness. You now have several boxes and bags and each has a destination. Don't leave them there. See the process through. Here are the steps to take:

Take the *Keep* box then decide whether you wish to work from that box or put back the things you've decided will stay in the room you've cleaned. If you desire simply to put them back in place, you can either do that now or take a break and return to it.

The *Keep* box will have some items you've decided to keep but don't belong in the room you decluttered. It's all right now to put those items in the appropriate rooms. If you haven't yet worked on that room, either put it away or store it in a closet until you can get to work on that room.

Trash and *recycle* boxes must now be placed in their normal days, pending the arrival of municipal services.

If you're not able at this point to take your *donate* box to the donation center, at least get them into your car now. You'll no doubt pass by in the next few days.

The *Sell* box has some "land mines." Until you're prepared to hold your yard sale, this box continues to be clutter. Worse, you may decide that you don't want to sell them items at all, which merely reintroduces them into your possessions. They were clutter then; they're still clutter. If you have the chance to turn something into money, do so. Even an ad on Craigslist might be a worth consideration.

What's Next?

What you've read is the decluttering overview. Now for some detail about what and how. Let's change our period to a half-hour. Let's see what we can do to each room in thirty minutes to bring some order to your home that will be pleasing to the potential buyer. You may even wish to retain this system once you have occupied a new home.

The Kitchen

Cabinets and Storage: You need to decide here whether the insides of your cabinets will be painted. If so, you may wish to remove completely the contents to permit that. Take an empty translucent plastic bin; get out the trash bin, a damp rag, a dry rag, or some paper towels. Inside each cabinet, one at a time, remove trash and throw it in the trash bin. What possible trash could reside in our cabinets? Nearly empty food and spice containers, for example; leftover packaging that you "might be able to use someday"—things you haven't used for a long time. Look carefully at your counters to determine whether some things that hadn't made it back to the cabinets can be placed in the bin.

If you choose not to empty the cabinets pending painting, now you must decide whether things in your cabinets belong elsewhere. Put them in the empty bin. Straighten what's there, wipe the shelf area with the damp rag, and dry with a dry rag or paper towels.

Do your cabinets one at a time. If you try to clean them all out, all you'll do is to clutter the counters or a table, making restoration more difficult. When you have completed the discard and cleaning tasks, now you can replace the items from your bin to the proper storage position.

Evaluate your appliance storage. If you have color-coordinated appliances, you may wish for them to remain on your counter-top, but at least arrange them for their best utility and hide their power cords. If you choose to stow some in cabinets, make them as easily accessible as possible, such that when the door is open the appliance is presented in showcase style—not merely crammed in with pots and pans. And about pots and pans: you may have liked your selection of eight fry pans and four or six covered pots, et al, when you bought them, and you'll like them again in your new home. Until this house is sold, put back to the smallest number you need to prepare most meals and pack the rest for storage or shipment.

Open the refrigerator. What can you throw away? You have fruit and vegetable bins—are they used for their purpose? Arrange your shelves for the items the appliance contains. Give the inside and outside a good cleaning.

Go into a supermarket after the shelves have been stocked for the next decluttering example. Note that the shelves are "square-faced," i.e., the product has at least the front row where all the jars and bottles are faced frontward and stacked neatly. That's what your cabinets should look like while you're preparing your home to be sold.

Then, when you've located things that don't belong in the kitchen, move them to the room where they belong. If that room has already been decluttered, introduce the returned item into the presentation scheme you have selected.

Kitchens and bathrooms are the rooms of most interest for a buyer, at least for the partner most involved. The sale of a property at a significant price will be seriously affected by the condition and presentation of these two rooms.

The Bathrooms

Bathroom clutter happens. It is a smaller room than others in the house. Things get pushed into small cabinets tucked into alcoves above and beneath the porcelain appliances. Magazines and other reading materials occupy counters and tank tops. Toothbrush holders, bar soap trays, cosmetic dispensers, brushes, hair dryers, and combs all are set on counter-tops. If you do not now have a good selection of bathroom storage solutions, you need to acquire some and to sort and organize the items in your bathroom.

Here is a trick to decluttering your bathrooms that you can do in a half hour or less if, once started, you are consistent with your process. Clear counter-tops and put the most-used daily items in the top drawers of vanities or under-sink cabinets.

Where do you keep your clothes hamper? If it's in the bathroom, put soiled towels, facecloths, hanging clothes, and other items that might need to be moved to where you do your laundry. Empty the hamper then go back to the bathroom and use it as a bin, into which you will place things that don't belong in the bathroom: the jewelry that you should have placed on a bedroom dresser, for instances. Perhaps clothes in the bathroom should be returned to a closet.

Clear and clean the counter-top near the sink. Replace items from place. Do the same in vanity or cabinet drawers and in under-the-sink storage. If your bathroom is large enough to have a linen closet, then make it pretty—simply make it attractive. A buyer will open the door—plan on it. Linen closets hold towels, comforters, sheets, and even surplus pillows and tablecloths. The problem is that we don't want to let go of anything. You may need a couple of extra pillows; you don't need six. You might occasionally need a comforter, but that can be placed on the top shelf at the back, where you might have to get a stepladder to retrieve it. Tubs, dividers, and small bins can handle much of the clutter in the linen closet.

If you were to evaluate carefully what your medicine cabinet contains, how much of it would be older than two or three months? Might you be wise to unload outdated items? You don't really need the six tubes of toothpaste you bought on sale in your medicine cabinet or giant bottles of rubbing alcohol, for example. You don't need a six-month supply of Q-Tips, bathroom tissue, or tissues in boxes. You may wish to store some in a cabinet in your basement, but put into the bathroom only what you will use in a short period. Organize that vanity. Store items in bins and jars. Things that do not stack well belong in bins.

Things "wander" in the bathroom. Brushes you put into a drawer often finish on the counter. A good way to handle this is with a holder designed to hold cosmetic pencils, mascara, and combs—or at least a wide-mouthed jar. Small bins that can be stored under the sink can organize some of what you know you must have available.

Then put the hamper back where it belongs, awaiting the next change of clothes.

The Dining Room

The kitchen or dining room table is a favorite place to stack stuff. When stuff is stacked there, the space becomes useless and you finish eating off TV trays positioned in front of the television in the family room. Aside from the fact that you know it should be used for its primary purpose—eating—you're now faced with ensuring that it at least appears to be used for its purpose.

It's not our purpose here to tell you how to use your kitchen table as a formal dining room. Rather, it is to help make it look as if the maid and the butler performed nightly duties in your home—and to find a way to get rid of the clutter.

All eating rooms have something in common: a table and a seating area. Here you will socialize, do some paperwork, or work on homework. The idea is to keep that table clear most of the time and certainly when you' show your home to a prospect.

If what's normally on the table (perhaps at one end) is paperwork, make the same decisions as you would in your home office: keep/file/shred/destroy. If the table has become a repository for schoolbooks and other miscellany, what you have discovered is that these items have no natural "home." You need either to find another more permanent location or discard them, which will make your child nervous if he or she is charged with returning schoolbooks.

If you have a formal dining room, you need to deal with china and glassware, silver or other tableware, and table linens—napkins, and tablecloths. Miscellaneous items, such as candlesticks or centerpieces belong there, as well. They will be part of the display process when the house is shown. Because those things belong there doesn't mean they should all *be* there. If you family is four, the balance of the utensil set and the excess number of table lines might better be stored in a nearby hall closet. Older homes have a breakfront or buffet where some glassware and extra dishes, and perhaps a modicum of linen can be stored. If your dining area has a sideboard, put there only the things you will use daily, and keep it clear otherwise. Perhaps, now that you have been married several years, you might be able to donate/discard that hideous cake knife that your mother-in-law gave you. She won't miss it.

The storage of "stuff" is a problem here, as well, if the table is a multiuse item, largely because when you want to eat from it, it's necessary to clear off the homework, sewing, newspaper, or whatever you're doing during that time. Typically, dining rooms, even formal dining rooms, don't have much built-in storage. That makes sideboards, buffets, and serving carts and tables important. If you have a closet in the room, then the suggestions made above for closets with dividers also apply. Some folks put dressers with dresser-scarves over them in their dining rooms.

If you have dining room furniture that has shelves and drawers, part of the clutter can be to display pleasing items and neatly fold linens into drawers. If you have china cabinets, corner cabinets, and hutches, they should not be cluttered. Things specifically family-oriented should be packed and replaced with minimum decoration.

What's on the walls of the dining room? Pictures of scenery. Not family. Not plate collections. Minimalist. Minimalist, please.

Table pads, if they're used, should be stowed from the way and the table left with a centerpiece and perhaps candles. Heavy linens can be folded neatly and placed in drawers, or can be placed on large hangers designed for the purpose. You can store them in a hall closet adjacent to the dining room.

The Living Room

Decluttering a living room is easy. In a living room often are bookshelves. Books go on bookshelves. You may wish to decrease the number of books displayed, packing the balance pending your move.

Living rooms (and/or) family rooms are often where entertainment electronics are used, and therefore are stored. The TV, of course, a DVD player, sound systems, and remotes tend to gather with similar kinds and often occupy a devoted place in the room. If you haven't a remote holder, get one. If not, then keep a small box into which they will be placed when the systems are shut down.

Get out the bin. Keep the most recent copy of magazines and toss the rest. The same is true for catalogs and miscellaneous mail that has found its way to the room. Straighten and restack books, DVDs, CDs, etc. You don't have to put candelabra on the piano, but a good covering of furniture polish wouldn't hurt.

Hang all clothes that find their ways over chair backs. Hall closets or hall trees will do for outerwear. Put other in the appropriate rooms, and the next time you are in that room, put them away. Did you drag a blanket with you when you nestled down by the fireplace? Take it back to the bedroom.

If you have a fireplace, it needs cleaning after every use. Not knowing when the next FSBO customer will call, then prepare the logs for the next fire when this one has cooled, perhaps on the following day. If you are fortunate enough to have a gas log, at least vacuum the firebox periodically.

Vacuum the floor regularly, and certainly before any potential customer arrives. From the longer perspective, if you still have an outdated carpet bring it up to date, particularly if you have animals. Does anybody remember shag carpeting? If you intend to keep the carpeting in the house you want to sell, arrange for a thorough cleaning. Inform the professional carpet cleaner if you have pets. If you do have pets, then have the entire house done. It leaves the house fresh as a daisy.

Bedrooms

Somewhat akin to closets are bedrooms, not only because bedrooms have closets, but also because a cluttered bedroom is a catchall. So grab a basket and gather things that don't belong there. Ultimately, these things must be returned to their proper places. Included are clothes that should be hung. You don't want a prospective buyer to see his pants hung on a book over the door or her bathrobe tossed over a vanity chair. For the clothes to be hung in a bedroom closet, it is not unusual to have "his" and "her" closets, or at least sides to a closet behind a double door. Arrangement here is key. Coats should be hung together, as should pants, shirts. Rearrange the closet until things are not only organized but appear to the viewer as "soldiers in a row," according to colors or sizes, or styles—your option. A prospect may not care *how* you organize. A prospect may care much that you *have* organized.

Of course, the bed should be made and duvets, comforters, or blankets pleasingly presented, pillows fluffed, throw pillows arranged. Miscellaneous furniture should accent the room with a unique focus, appropriately festooned with throw pillows. Again, remember that we're preparing to sell. The logic of removing collections and pictures holds here, as well. Anything brought into a bedroom or a guest room that does not belong there must be relocated to its proper place.

Are there dressing tables or bedside tables? Make them neat! Dress them up. Put the boxes of tissue in their unique container, for example. Keep cosmetics and nail instruments from sight. If a bathroom is located off the master bedroom, the bathroom considerations previously stated still apply, though you might get away with hanging a snow-white bathrobe on a hook at the back of the bathroom door.

Closets and Storage

Would it not be nice to have more storage room than we need and to put things into seasonal or functional closets? If your home is blessed to have a cedar closet, then you're aware of the kind of clothes that should be hung there. If you have a gigantic walk-in closet where "his" suits and sport jackets, trousers and shirts can be hung in splendor and where "her" blouses, dresses, skirts, and shoes—let's not forget the shoes—can be organized, then you are fortunate. Many homes built through the years solved the closet storage problems with summer and winter closets and things were rotated upon the advent of the season.

For most of us, there are one, or possibly two, clothes closets, plus one "hall closet," where we hang the coats of guests, at least those of us who don't dump them on the bed in the master bedroom.

Many of us simply buy too many clothes. At some point, the closets become congested. Only with reluctance will many of us give up on a favorite jacket, suit, dress, or robe. Nevertheless, if that closet is full of things you no longer wear, it's time for you to remove some. You'll know that's the case when the shirt or blouse comes wrinkled from the closet or you simply cannot find something that you're certain that you put in there.

If you have children, then hand-me-down items have some utility in your family, at least among children of the same gender. It's a fact, though it can't be defended by numbers, that not much clothing is sold during a yard sale. It's equally a fact that discarded clothing, donated to a rescue mission, can have some resale value—to the benefit of the mission's customers and clients. Those items not used by the rescue charity can still derive funds from bundlers who ship low-priced but serviceable clothing overseas to third-world countries.

So what to remove and/or donate? Clothing that no longer pleases you. Clothing that no longer fits you. Clothing that is no longer in style. Clothing that is simply surplus: how many pairs of jeans does one person need? Fad clothing, like "torn" jeans, will eventually no longer be in vogue. It's time to let these items go. Closet space is limited and you know that things hung neatly will be far more attractive to a prospective buyer.

That doesn't mean it will be easy. Perhaps one of the items is the dress your daughter graduated from high school in. Neither you nor she will ever wear it again, but it holds sentimental value. Or perhaps the business suit that you paid so much for is there and you'll be darned if you'll let something so expensive go to the mission. Go there and look; you'll see many designer labels. Of course, you're convinced that eventually you'll need it, but face it—your life has changed. By that time, you'll have gained and lost lots of clothes.

Declutter your closets by buying storage solutions that maximize space. Want ideas? Go to CaliforniaClosets.com or to Solutions-Store.ca. Visit a storage products store. Be sure to carry your closet measurements with you.

Storage Solutions

One way to get more storage from your closet space it is with double hangs. The concept of double hangs is to raise the top bar far enough for a second bar to be placed beneath them. Look into wire closet shelving at your home products stores.

Valet hooks will give you small quantity temporary hanging space. The Command Hooks from 3M will allow you to place a hook where it's needed and remove it at will.

While wire may be good for hanging clothes in a closet, it's not at all good for heavier clothing. Wire hangers, such as come from the dry cleaners, are not suitable for permanent storage. Suits, blazers, dresses, pants, shorts, all could have specialized hangers, but a simple wooden hanger will be sufficient. In addition of providing shape and structure for your clothes (and they differ men's from women's), visually they present a well-organized picture for anyone opening the closet.

Shelf dividers keep things from mixing. Folded clothes, such as shirts, sweaters, and jeans look neat, and especially so in a closet used by more than one person. They come in colors and you can position them according to the size of your clothes.

We've discussed plastic containers. They belong in closets, as well. They are see-through and allow ease of identification. They also provide protection from moisture and excessive airflow. If you place like items together, it will not be necessary to label them.

Plastic baskets and bins allow you to place like items together then extract them from a closet shelf, work with the contents, then replace them. They're a good place for scarves, belts, items of underwear, etc.

The Home Office

Your home office is a large empty barrel. You open your mail, scan it, and lay it down on your desk. You continue to do that until you gather a pile of correspondence. You hope you can casually remove mail that you do not wish to read and discard it, and other items, such as empty envelopes.

The desk catches everything: books to read, bills to pay, messages that have arrived in your absence, and somewhere under the pile is your calendar or appointment book.

Also on the desk, you have one or more computers, one or more monitors, a telephone, and a stapler, a roll of tape, various writing instruments, and the pictures of your daughter last year at Disney World.

What if this was your work desk and your firm had a rule that all desks had to be clear when you leave for the night—except the computer screen, of course?

A good way to declutter a home office is to establish your procedures first then abide by them. Here are some ideas:

Unless you have many clients, having a filing cabinet of customer folders isn't a wise idea. Put together some categorical folders then use them according to function:

As you go through your mail, treat each piece when you open it. File the envelope in the wastebasket—now. If you need to record the return address, simply tear it away from the envelope. Then update it and any changes of address you receive.

Remove the junk mail—avoid opening it simply because you're curious. Get it off your desk. If you recycle flat paper, put it in a recycling container.

If what is on your desk hasn't been used today, stow it. Keep a mental record of how often that item comes from the drawer. How many pens and pencils do you need?

Do you need storage that isn't available in a cabinet? Do-it-yourself cabinets can be obtained or shelving placed against an unused office wall.

Cut your paper input. Get your statements online. Instruct your service providers and banks to use email where possible. Then you can print what you need and store the rest for future use.

Keep your own printing to a minimum. Use e-mail or other electronic transmission where possible. Occasionally, we print "junk," things printed in error or which, for some reason, must be reprinted. Use the back of such printing for scratch pads or for printing that's for internal use only.

As with your closets, there are people whose business is workflow design. Don't fear investigative help. In the short term, the idea is to make the place look neat and inviting to a prospective buyer.

Office chairs and tables are often the receptacles for things we wish we had time to read. If you haven't generated the time to read, then don't pack in the magazines. Look at them and any bound reports, pick what you want from them, scan the pages into your computer, and then discard the magazines. The same can be said for books, but book can be held temporarily on office shelving—after your relocate.

Finally, get rid of the junk. Your old Radio Shack TRS-80 might be a museum piece at this point, but those who need it for that already have it. Anymore, electronic equipment costs more to repair than to replace. Find a way to recycle it. If it's old but still productive, find a public school that wants it and donate it.

In an era of rampant identity threats, one good decluttering advice is to acquire a shredder. Shredders are available in models that mangle single sheets through those that can handle several sheets at once. They can hang over wastebaskets or be obtained with bins where the sliced paper is gathered. Here's what you might consider shredding: the general rule is anything with account numbers, birth dates, maiden names, passwords and pins, signatures, and social security numbers.

Here are some things you should shred: ATM receipts, bank statements, birth certificates, canceled and voided checks, credit-card bills, credit reports, expired identify cards, expired passports and visas, investment account numbers and transactions, legal documents, anything you've signed, passwords and pin numbers, anything with identification of you, anything with identifying account numbers, tax forms, used tickets, and utility bills. There may be more.

The Laundry Room

The most cluttered area in your house has to be your laundry room. This is where the baskets of dirty clothes finish, and chances are that you have at least two washings to do at any time: whites and colored. An efficient laundry room would provide closet storage for cleaning supplies, some form of washer—and dryer—and perhaps even some portable clothesline for those things to be hand-washed or dry naturally. A multi-bin hamper, permanently positioned in the laundry room, would be a wise purchase. That way, traveling hampers can be quickly emptied and sorted, then removed. Keep the selection of cleaning products to a minimum, sticking with all-purpose formulations.

If you could engage a designer for this bathroom, chances are that you now have a room where the utilities are appropriately organized and where excessive steps are cut to a minimum. Designs of laundry facilities place this room either in a larger bathroom or adjacent to water lines. You may even have a "broom closet," where the broom, dust mop, wet mop, buckets, sponges, and vacuum cleaner lives. You might even have a built-in ironing board.

Whatever you have, you face two tasks for use and one important task for decluttering. For use, facilitate the movement of dirty clothes into the room and clean/dry ones from the room. If it doesn't have to dry naturally, carry your hampers there, do the wash, move the clean clothes to the dryer, and remove when the buzzer goes off. Then get the clothes back to the closets where they will reside, careful to fold, hang, and arrange the items for the inevitable inspection.

Laundry rooms generate trash—things removed from pants pockets, for example, and "fuzz" from the lint traps. They are a magnet for things that don't belong there. You brought a book to read while the machines were working. Is it still there? Do you use the closets there for things that belong elsewhere—the garden hose, miscellaneous tools, sports items? Read the book, but remove it when you're through, and all those other things, as well, especially when you wish to show the house. Make a point of keeping things out that don't belong there and removing things carried in for temporary use.

If you have a counter-top or shelves, use small bins to store temporarily things from pockets, miscellaneous single socks, clothespins, small tools, and periodically used brushes.

The Garage

"Clean out the garage"—the siren song of every junk collector who's ever lived. The garage is the ultimate "free-form" storage facility. It's a place originally designed to hold vehicles. Ultimately, it degenerates to the place everything that seems not to belong to elsewhere finishes. It's a curiosity, and you will find people who leave their automobiles outdoors because there's no room in the garage. Decluttering the garage for your FSBO will be fun, if for no other reason than you will be forced to throw away/donate/sell stuff. It's the last space in the home that you should declutter. Why? Because much of what you decluttered from inside the home has finished here. Recall that it was recommended that some inside's contents could be packed for storage. Ideally, you should contemplate renting a storage locker in the short-term.

Sell Your Own Home

When a garage becomes cluttered, it's often because you really haven't accepted that some things there really belong elsewhere, and you haven't taken the time to put the items away. It's "free form" largely because (other than your automobiles) they are items of diverse sizes and weights and you couldn't move them elsewhere if you wanted to, unless you happen to have a garage that opens on your basement, in which case you've multiplied the problem.

There's one more dimension. Houses are not often built with decorated garages. Generally, the walls are framed and sheathed but remain open on the inside. Now you have a fundamental question to be answered: would it be worthwhile to invest money in the garage to help the sale? Actually, Another question: why in the world would you do that now, since you hadn't bothered to do it at all while you lived there? The solution to the entire dilemma is that a minor amount of investment can raise the selling price significantly. It's all in the cosmetics.

Over time, you have structured your garage. You may have some shelves there, perhaps also a workbench. It has become the place your trash receptacles live. You may have used some space for storage of snow machines, bicycles, flammable fluids, etc. If you want to completely rework your garage, that's one thing. At the least, it's time to come to grips with how the place looks.

So take a weekend—at least consecutive days. Pick a dry weekend, because some accumulation will no doubt finish in the driveway temporarily. Get some help—a friend, neighbor, relative, or that teenage boy who lives at your house. This person will help move bulky items and will accelerate the process, simply to see it completed in the shortest time possible. It would be useful to do a little planning before you begin.

Among the things you should plan would be the groupings. Put your camping gear together in one place. Likewise, your gardening tools. Do you have auto shop tools there? Gather them, as well, and if you have a built-in workbench, perhaps you can put them there.

Don't plan to put things on shelves right away. Empty the shelves. If you've the piece-together shelving, consider building some static shelving. If you already have static shelving, consider reworking it to make it appear uniform. If you have the time, a coat of paint might be a wise investment.

You will need storage containers, but don't get them yet. Many items in your garage are heavier in weight. Make sure you know what sizes your shelving can accommodate and how sturdy those containers must be. In the short term, some miscellaneous cardboard boxes will be useful.

If you have loose miscellaneous hardware—bolts, nuts, washers, screws, wall anchors, etc., obtain multiple-drawer containers that will allow their organization. You should be doing that all along, so continue that during the decluttering process.

Chances are that you have several paint cans of varying sizes, each of which contain little paint. You chose to keep them "in case something needs touching up." Now is the time to get those into the trash. What you keep from your garage may well depend on where you intend to ultimately reside. You may wish to keep the artificial Christmas tree (get it onto a shelf), but you may be moving to a place you'll have no need for snow tires. Put them up for sale.

Sitting on the bench or in large tool boxes are your auto and carpenter tools. Take all loose tools and find ways to store them in the toolboxes, in wall brackets, or on pegboards. You'll need the tools. You probably won't need the old muffler that fell off last winter. Is there a metal recycling plant in your locale? Start your donation and trash piles now, and put them right in the middle of the garage floor, meaning that you will have to deal with them before you can bring the cars back into the garage.

Plan how you would like the garage to appear when you're done. While your things are on the floor or in the driveway, now is the time to sheathe the inside of the garage, building in the shelves that will appear. This might take a second weekend or continue into a stretch of good weather, but with a little effort and a little expenditure, you can make the property more attractive. Find a prospect that does his auto repair, and this will help seal the deal.

If your garage is structured to permit an "attic" of sorts, with load-bearing joists that will permit a "floor" to be attached, that will provide some storage ability. Allow enough room near the door to store trash and recycling receptacles and places to hang rakes, shovels, and brooms. That's for decluttering the garage. Now let's look at things you might do to enhance the garage—*while it is empty.*

In what shape is the garage floor? If you live where salt and calcium are spread on the roads during the winter, your garage floor will show it, as both interact with the concrete there. Now is the time to clean it thoroughly, contract to have the surface epoxied and painted to permit a smooth satin or glossy surface.

Comparative Analysis on Home Repairs

In the US, *Remodeling Magazine* publishes an annual cost vs. value report. That shows features and several home project costs and returns in four regions, including a national average. See www.remodeling.hw.net/cost-vs-value/2020/**. In Canada, it's www.cmhc-schl.gc.ca/en/hoficlincl/homain/stda/index.cfm.

Repairs to Furnaces, Water Heaters, and A/C Units

Most people want to buy a perfect home. To achieve your greatest return, focus on the obvious and those with a useful life. Look first at the furnace and water heater.

If you're beyond the life of the unit, consider replacement. Your potential buyers will, and their offers will anticipate that both will fail shortly after they move in. You may finish paying for a repair either from pocket or in a deduction from your closing settlement. Ensure all the units and any cooling systems that may be a part of the home, have been inspected, maintained, and certified as working satisfactorily.

Repairs to the home's systems should be done by professionals: plumbers, electricians, or gas workers. Modern designs may be more energy efficient. Modernizing and can pay dividends on your FSBO.

Paint the Ceilings and Walls

Stains on the ceilings can indicate a leaky roof. Smoke gathers on the kitchen ceiling and move throughout the house. New paint freshens everything. It is a most cost-effective home improvement. Pick the pleasant but neutral color paint.

Wallpaper was your choice—not the buyer's. Rent a wall steamer and take the paper off before painting the walls. Should you paint over the wallpaper? No.

Wood paneling in walnut, mahogany, cedar, and pine is passé. Prime it and paint it in soft, neutral colors.

Textured ceilings need to be stripped. It's not expensive but it does take some time. Do that before you repaint the ceiling.

Increases in lighting are of great benefit. New drapery or blinds will help. Find a way to admit as much sunlight as possible. If you expect to leave the drapes, put them in a closet.

Apply that fresh look concept to your bedroom. If you have a walk-in closet, put light colors on the walls there, also. The idea is to create the illusion of space.

Flooring Fixes

Older homes may have hardwood floors, probably in oak. Later homes had carpet over plywood. Remove any shag carpeting. Choices in laminates and carpeting abound and are relative inexpensive.

However, if hardwood floors are under that carpet, rip up and discard the carpet. Find a service to sand and refinish the floors.

With plywood under the carpet, you would be wise to change the carpet, preferably in a neutral color. Before the carpet is laid, check for "play" in the plywood against the floor joists and nail them down.

Ceramic floors or granite tiles get chipped or cracked. If you can afford to replace the damaged tiles, do so, particularly in hallways and entryways. In other places, see carpet, above.

Kitchen Repairs and Improvements

Small kitchens beg for light colors on the cabinetry. You're looking to enlarge the image of the kitchen. Hang wall-mounted racks and holders to keep the counter space clear

Nearly everything in the kitchen has a large price tag. If you have expensive appliances, you probably won't realize their full (even depreciated) cost. If they are not uniform in color, arrange to have them painted identically.

Kitchen remodels, particularly of replaced or refinished cabinets, will return most of their costs in elevated property values. Resurfacing may be your best option. New veneers and door replacements might do it. Paint them with soft and neutral colors, contrasted with wall colors. Use new and contrasting hardware with accentuate the cabinets.

You don't have to install granite counters. New laminates with splashguards are a nice touch. New faucets and sparkling sinks will help your sale.

Bathrooms

The bathroom needs to be perfect—period. Ensure sinks, tubs, showers, and other porcelain surfaces are not nicked. Upgrade the bathroom to include new and stylish faucets, knobs, and towel racks. If you coordinate everything, the look appears modern.

The same concern should be held for plumbing and fixtures as with the kitchen fixtures. What you would recoup from a bathroom remodel is only about two-thirds of its cost. However, new floors, changed fixtures, and improved lighting will pay.

Roof Inspections

You probably cannot repair your own roof, to say nothing about the safety concerns. Have a competent roofer evaluate your roof and make necessary changes. This will be subject to a home inspection effort, and you'll face making the changes anyway. You'll be inconvenienced, to be sure, but buyers shy from poorly maintained roofs. A new roof becomes an assurance of quality in the FSBO arena.

Exterior

We'll discuss property exteriors when we discuss "curb appeal." In the short term, if your sidewalk has cracks, they must be patched. Likewise, your asphalt driveways. The fences need to be in repair and have new paint. You might consider new caulking for windows and doors, new doors where necessary, and certainly a new coat of paint on them. Doorknob and lock hardware is like new fixtures in the bath and kitchen.

Replacing Older Plumbing and Wiring

If your house is older, before you sell it, you may wish to update your wiring and plumbing. Many older homes used aluminum wiring, and that kind has created problems. You may wish to replace with copper. Many older homes used polybutylene piping, and they are prone to leak. Again, you may wish to use copper. The most important concept here is that to do so the walls must be open. If you're replacing walls anyway, besides the wiring, check the plumbing.

Some plumbing repair tips: Before you interrupt your waterline, turn it off at the street or the meter. Open the taps to reduce line pressure. Put a bucket under every incision you make in the water line. Replace shut-off valves and install new ones where practical. If your stove is gas, install an electric line. If it is electric, install a gas line. Make it useful to the next purchaser. Get rid of all galvanized plumbing. Install water lines and shut-offs for the refrigerator now. Be sure to check for municipal codes if you attempt to do this work yourself. You do not want the sale of your house held up while things are redone by a licensed contractor. Another concern will be for new electric or lighting installations. Municipal code departments can provide the rules for various forms of lighting.

Ensuring that electrical updating is done by a licensed contractor would be wise. Older houses were often built with 60-amp services. Over time, the electrical needs blossomed and some of those services were upgraded to 100-amps. Today, a 200-amp service is necessary in any home. Before you do that, however, spend time with an electrical contractor in your area. Separate circuits are needed for stoves, refrigerators, and microwave units.

Many kitchen remodels involve recessed ceiling lighting, new pendants, and / or breakfast nook lighting. Check with your city code department to learn its requirements for incandescent, fluorescent and halogen bulbs. In the kitchen, many of these items may be on your list:

- Lighting for beneath the cabinets or over the sink.
- Overhead lighting, with recessed fixtures.
- Wiring for the dishwasher and garbage disposal.
- Wiring the garbage disposal, either directly or by plugging into a receptacle.
- Wiring necessary for a kitchen range.

- Receptacle for the refrigerator.
- Wiring for the range hood.
- Receptacle for the microwave.
- Several countertop receptacles.
- Dimmer switches for this and for other rooms, as well.

Other Improvements and Repairs

Screened doors, windows, and seasonal rooms: Anything in disrepair outside of your house will be a red flag to a potential buyer. After a while, aluminum doors and windows sag, and they're not easily repaired. The wise FSBO seller sells them for the metal and installs new ones. Before you do so, however, you may find that the screws—which are steel, not aluminum—are simply rusted or loose. Going over the aluminum with a screwdriver would be a wise investment of time.

Let Dead Plants Rest in Peace . . . Elsewhere

Of course, if you want your home to appear the best, mow the lawn. Go around your flowerbeds, if you have them, and pull weeds and dead plants. Clip dead blossoms and stems. You may never have raked the lawn, depending on the mulcher to fine-chop the grass. While your home is for sale, you must rake everything then dispose of the yard waste away from your property.

Paint the Front Door

Unless you have a heavy oak wooden door on the front of your house that you would prefer to stain, paint the door a color that stands out. Be careful here: psychedelic pink stands out, but you don't want it. You do want a warm, conservatively colored front door. Consider deep greens, deep blues, and black, though your house may be white.

Make the Roof "Neat"

A single look at the roof accompanied by a roofer's testimony as to its soundness may be sufficient to assuage any roof fears. You want that buyer to concentrate on how he or she will furnish your home to belong there. Get a roofing contractor to remove any moss and possibly treat the roof for future moss with zinc carbonate.

Gutter Treatments

Gutters are built to allow water to flow from your roof to the ground without running down the siding of your house and carrying dissolved dirt onto the surface. Gutter work is something you can do—on a clear, dry day. Done when the weather is warm, the task isn't difficult. Clear out the leftover leaves, the sand debris that has run off the shingles, and any other accumulated debris.

When you set up the ladder, carry the hose, and rinse it out. Watch the end-caps and joints on the downspouts while it drains. If the caps leak, once the system has dried, apply caulking, using butyl caulking. Use a caulking gun to press the sealer into place and don't fear getting your fingers dirty.

Patch and Paint

If you can afford to repaint the outside of your home, then do so. If you're not familiar with a compressed paint gun, then hire the work done.

Painting inside is something that you can do alone, with adequate time, a little skill, and much patience. Mostly what you'll patch will be nail holes, where you have hung pictures. Small holes can be filled in with soap, primed, and repainted. Moderately sized holes can be patched with wall putty, sanded, primed, and repainted. Larger holes require a qualified repairman with appropriate knowledge. If you try to do them yourself, buyers will wonder what you're hiding.

Deodorize

If your house has been a haven for smokers or animals, you'll need to do some extra work. We've already mentioned that carpet cleaners have a solution to apply to rugs. If you house has had mold, then you must do some remedial work.

Cigarette/cigar smoke not only gathers on ceilings, it gathers on walls, and nicotine. Over time, those walls will yellow. You will need to wash them with ammonia. You will need to seal cracks and deep clean with bleach, regrout tiles and recaulk cracks. The best advice is not to try to cover those smells with fragrances from candles, potpourri, and room fragrancers. Cover the walls with Kilz primer (seals in smells) then paint them. Air the place out and replace the filters in your heating and air-conditioning systems.

If you have pets, some odor of those pets lingers in carpets and draperies. Discuss a high ozone shock treatment with the person who cleans carpets. The treatment takes about an hour and has a positive effect on mold, as well.

Minor Wood Surface Repairs

If you choose not to paint your woodwork and worn cabinets, improve their look with scratch covers and polish. Old English makes separate formulations for light or dark wood and does it in stick form. It is colored oil and because of that may appear shiny at the point of repair. A good lemon furniture polish will spread that.

Cosmetic Repairs

Of course, systems that don't work need help. If your sink drains don't work, find the reason, and you may need to disassemble traps and clean the pipes. If your toilet isn't draining well, then you need to clear a blockage with a plunger, a chemical compound, or a "snake."

For the majority of things, throw rugs are a blessing. Well-applied cleaners and touchups can overcome the appearance of more complicated problems. It's not that the buyer fears the problem, but it is that the appearance of a problem causes a buyer to think twice about what may not be obvious.

Staging your home for the quickest sale

The idea of staging your home is far more than cleaning it up, painting it throughout, and cutting the grass. For the balance of the chapter, we will discuss ways to make your home most presentable by painting a picture attractive to a homebuyer. Staging is merchandising your home. Realtors refer to it as "home fluffing."

By definition, home staging optimizes a home's appeal to the largest number of prospects, using a variety of techniques to remove you and the impact of your possessions from your home (whether you do empty the house). The idea is to make sweeping and subtle changes that will lead to a fast and profitable sale. You can do it yourself or you can hire a professional stager to do it for you. It's a function of your skills.

By now, you've decided to let the house go, have said good-bye to your favorite view or room, and have done the maintenance necessary to ensure your house "works," not only for you, but also for a potential purchaser.

Here are a couple of things you might never have considered:

Fresh and fragrant flowers make the dining room warm and inviting.

A freshly ground lemon in the garbage disposal will create great aroma for your kitchen, and you don't have to have something in the oven when a prospect arrives.

Real houseplants add atmosphere. Don't overdo it. Don't use artificial plants.

Realize that your potential buyers don't wish to hear about problems—of any kind—the neighbors, the traffic, the community.

Please keep your visitors from your business. They need no introduction to your bank account, the bills you receive, or personal letters. It is welcome information if you can have a small collection of utility bills.

Wash the dishes and put them away. Do the laundry and put it away, as well.

Your prospects aren't interested to know how many repairs were done to make the house ready to sell or what they cost. That tells them that you were remiss in maintenance over time, and they'll wonder what exists that you're not telling them.

No new projects while the property is for sale. It would be wise to complete them before putting the house up for sale.

Board all pets for the duration and ensure all the feed bowls, anchor chains, and litter boxes are out of sight.

It's a Setup

Ideally, your home should be empty—totally. You should go somewhere until the house is sold if you wish to allow objective views and not take the chance of messing up the interaction or putting your possessions at risk. Chances are that won't happen. If the house is empty, then you have the option of obtaining cardboard furniture or possibly renting a paucity of furniture necessary to display the home.

Showcasing is what home staging is all about. When was the last time you worried about visually pleasing sightlines? Probably never. When was the last time you were concerned that the room had a focus? If the room was the one that had the TV, it might be the one, but a secondary concern for the living room that contains the TV is the fact that all the sitting surfaces are back to the room's entrance. You probably never worried about that.

We will offer some ideas about all this, but much publicly available knowledge is available about home staging and professionals who have made it their business to consult about how your home should be staged for sale. Caution alert: Dad's ratty old recliner is probably headed for the trash heap.

One thing we have learned is that any room—no matter what the room is—should limit the number of colors used in the room. We've also learned that a well-staged home sells quickly, easily, and often for more than others, often well more than the money it takes to make it happen. That might make staging a wise investment.

What about a Professional Stager?

Since moving out is probably not an option, recognize that living in your house differs from selling it. You house is now a "product." The quicker you can transform your house into an appealing "product," the faster you'll sell, and the more of your equity you can protect. Staging your house helps you achieve these goals. A professional stager can:

- Provide an objective analysis of the inside and outside of your house to see it through a buyer's eyes.

- Recommend ways to make the house look its best at the lowest cost, including any cosmetic repairs needed.

- Advise about what to pack and store.

- Recommend paint colors, when repainting is needed.

- Provide exterior detailing and curb appeal recommendations to make buyers want to come in and see more.

- Place furniture and accessories to create a "wow factor" that photographs well for MLS, online and print advertising, creating an inviting impression buyers will remember.

- Help set priorities for what *you* can do, and what will be most helpful.

- Recommend trades people and other resources.

This would give credence to involving a stager from where you decide to make the property FSBO. It's not cheap; hiring a consultant never is. You'll find rates that run from $75 per hour and up. Often the consultant will bid an entire job for a fixed price function. Rates for that could stretch into the thousands. If you own an estate, it might even be expressed in a percentage of the sale price. As stated before, the increase in the sale price because you have the services of a staging consultant should be more than sufficient to cover the cost.

It's Not WYSIWYG

The term WYSIWYG means "what you see is what you get." It was a popular term a few years back, largely for electronic publishing and comedian Flip Wilson's character Geraldine. Home staging is definitely not that—it's creating an illusion that will make your house look brighter, cleaning, warmer, and far more attractive than a thorough vacuuming, an entire coat of paint, and the pictures of you and your smiling puppies.

You've decluttered, repaired, painted, trimmed, arranged, neatened, organized, and said a prayer over your work. Staging is what you do next. It's clearing off the dozen cosmetic items from your dressing table and replacing them with a simple assortment of things that belong there. The key concept here is to make attractive by keeping it simple. About the dressing table—when you last used it, you may have had a dozen different tubes and jars, pencils and brushes, face and body creams, and a current copy of *People* magazine. When you're through, you may leave a comb, a lipstick, an eyebrow pencil, and mascara. The rest you will have secreted in the table's drawers, in neat organizing containers.

Think of a stager as an artist who will perceive your rooms as blank canvasses and will return to you a desirable portrait, having created images that appeal to the buyer's senses. Here are things they might do:

Arrange furniture groupings. The artist calls them a vignette. If you can picture a wineglass, a bottle of wine, and a dish of grapes, painted in oils on canvas, then perhaps you can also see that an appropriately placed couch, overstuffed chair, ottoman, and magazine rack becomes a part of a vignette. You've see pictures where with a chessboard set with the various pieces arranged. It was a vignette.

The artist may weave a picture in fabrics, creating attractive attention-focused objects with simple lines and colors. All those books that you packed will not leave shelf space for attractive knickknacks that draw a buyer's attention. If you have a fireplace, mirrors and mantels can become a focusing attraction. A creative stager does her work with mirrors, plants, silk flowers, floor & table lamps, area and throw rugs, ottomans, baskets, and anything that will demonstrate the utility of the room, sparsely presented, of course.

There is a collision of interests between a stager and an agent. As mentioned, the agent would like the home to be empty. To the stager, an empty home is cold and lifeless. Because it can be demonstrated that staging pays, the agent goes with the perspective—and you should, as well.

A stager will be interested that you oil the cabinets, place bowls of brightly colored fruit, vases of fresh flowers, and colorful cookbooks in the kitchen. She may feel differently about the grease-soaked Chilton Manual in the garage, but will insist that it at least appears presentable.

A stager will be interested in opening the bathrooms— good air circulation, beautiful colors, perhaps some small baskets filled with small ribbon-tied washcloths, scented soaps and creamy lotions. The important perspective here is organization. Don't let poor organization create more clutter.

The stager will be interested in the appearance of the outside of the house, as well. Beyond the recommendations made about painting and mowing, she will focus on decks, pools, and whatever garden features your home may offer.

You will find that stagers take many pictures—of the "before" and "after" kind. You will be able to see the difference. You may even wish to use the "after" pictures in your publicity.

Another side of the question: failure to stage your house means having to price at or near the bottom of its range to attract interest. You can never raise the price of your house; you can only reduce it. Several bidders for your property can cause the price to rise, but more often, it goes the other way. If the pictures published on your home are less attractive than they could be, particularly those that appear on the Internet—where most home buying begins today—then you'll be forced to start at a lower price, forfeiting money you could obtain. Remember, you do not have a second chance to make a first impression. You must WOW them! If you don't, you risk a longer time for the property to be on the market and a lower eventual selling price. A staging consultant is certainly worth of consideration. You can find them online or perhaps recommended by a local agent.

Can you do it yourself? Yes, of course. However, we're back to a fundamental question: can you afford to quit your job and simply work on your home until it sells? If you can, then you're golden and you can price at or near the top of the available range. Whatever you do yourself will help sell the house, but some participation by a professional stager is still a worthy investment.

Sell Your Own Home

So, How Do I Do It?

Some of this has been mentioned before, and because of that, less detail will be presented here:

Depersonalize. Until you're from this home and safely set in a new place, pack the family photos and heirlooms. The buyer was to picture his own photos and heirlooms in this home. Remove those things and the buyer will be led to place himself in the home.

Watch out for the interest and timing traps. Remove your diplomas, awards, wedding pictures, and other personal memorabilia. Anything that can produce bias will cause a reaction to somebody. If you sell used cars and the prospect hates used car salesmen, though entirely subconsciously, a bias is created. Wall hangings can demonstrate your financial position—pictures taken at your camp at a fancy lake, for example. Pictures taken at your daughter's christening might cause an unstated offense for a nonreligious person. Pictures taken of you at a rock festival might rankle someone who finds offense at the music. Whatever it is, don't take the chance. Subtlety can ruin objectivity.

Buyers are interested in built-in drawers and cabinets. They might open them; be sure you have removed personal items you wish other not to see. Don't give them an excuse to low-bid your sale.

The same is true for counters. Don't leave your mail there for inspection, and if you do decide to vacate pending the showing of your home, make sure somebody comes by to pick-up the mail that appears in your absence. If any of that mail indicates that you are in necessity for selling the property, the potential buyer will assume you're in a difficult position and offer less.

Do all the things previously mentioned for closets and cabinets. The key to this is organization and neatness. Buyers may open cabinet and closet doors, desiring to position mentally their belongings, but they will view what you have there. Think uniformity.

Rent a storage unit away from the home. You may not purchase cardboard furniture or rent furniture for showing, but you should understand that less is more concerning your own furniture. Pull some of it out and put it in storage. You may be willing to walk around a coffee table to get to the kitchen, but give the buyer the vision of a straight, unencumbered path. Leave appropriate things in their rooms, but get rid of a bunch of them, at least to a storage locker.

Remove from the house the things you don't want a buyer to see. Are those your favorite drapes? Did grandma bequeath you a Canada or Boston rocker that you intend to take? Remove anything you wouldn't be willing to sell to a buyer separately or which you would hate to lose should the buyer place a contingency upon it. Be rational—you may leave the family's upright piano because it accents the room. A baby grand is another matter. Store it or get a piano store to store it for you. It will have to be tuned at the next house anyway, but for now, it takes up much space.

Remove from the house any evidence of desperation to sell. Are you going through a divorce? Are your clothes in the closets and none from your spouse? Likewise, hobby items? She may still have her sewing machinery, but his woodshop is gone. The picture created is one of desperation. Avoid it where you can. You don't need to give away your motivation to move.

Sell Your Own Home

Creating a Focal Point

While you want the rooms to appear larger; while you want the colors to be light; while you want the airflow to be light and breezy, your staging efforts must also identify and create attention to the one place in the room to which you wish to draw attention. This focus will provide a specific center to define beauty or functionality.

What is a focus? It's what demands attention when the prospect walks into a room in your home. It may be décor; it may be functionality. Whatever it is, it must command attention, either subtly or directly. You don't want *a* focal feature—you want *the* focal feature that is most impressive.

A focus does not have to be an object in the room itself. It could even be the view out the window. Focal points, particularly those you choose to photograph and use for marketing, must create a mental image that either attracts them to look at the room or to visualize it after the fact. The focus could be a garish painting, but the better focus defines the usefulness of each space. While we aren't necessarily seeking the center of the room, we are seeking the center of attention for that room.

Some Examples

Bedrooms: you use a bedroom to rest; ergo the focus must be the bed. While you are holding the home up for sale, high quality, visually attractive bed dressing must be used.

Dining rooms denote fellowship—warm, friendly time spent with acquaintances and loved ones. It's the place you break bread. The table and chairs must be the focus, and chair scarves used with formal dining rooms offer a touch of elegance.

Media rooms must focus on the things to be seen, perhaps on a wide screen. If the media room doubles as a game room, you would be wise to deemphasize that and any possible appurtenances that identify the place as the "man cave," such as sports memorabilia.

Living and family rooms are for visiting. Conversation is what generally happens there. With a fireplace, show the grouping of furniture focused on that fireplace. If not, then a furniture orientation becomes the focus. Do not, repeat, do not take pictures of Junior sprawled out on a couch texting his only love.

Rules for focal points: Each space is unique. If your home has a "great room," you may need to identify several foci there. Several space divisions and the groupings therein will demonstrate the scale of the interior space and the multipurpose utility of those spaces.

Curb Appeal

Curb appeal is what your neighbors see daily. It's what a prospect sees when he drives up in front of your home. Included in curb appeal will be such things as lighting, color, lawn, shrubbery, walkways, asphalt driveway, flowers, and trees. If what the prospect sees is warm and inviting, you'll have many requests to see. Some of those will be agents who work with FSBO sellers.

Again, you don't get a second chance to make a first impression. A buyer wants to like what he or she sees on the outside before inquiring into the inside. If the buyer is pleased, there is a positive attitude toward the rest on the home. Depending on the weather, colorful and attractive plans say, "Come see me." Inviting doormats, a newly painted front door, large house numbers that stand out against the color of the home, and perhaps outstanding hardware will all whisper the message, one by one, as the prospect is drawn to the home.

Curb appeal is highly important. The beauty of finding curb appeal is that unless you have a landscaper on retainer, you can do much of the work yourself. Start by pulling and thinning vegetation. A mowed and well-trimmed lawn shows neatness and organization. Pulling weeds from between pieces of concrete will help overlook the fact that the driveway hasn't been well maintained. Gardens before and behind all add to the value of the home, if they are maintained, as will well-maintained trees spaced proportionately around the property. The vegetation, all well-watered, will require attention, but can be a selling feature to the person for whom the outside of the house is important.

Exterior lighting is a plus. Carriage lights by the front door give an essence of grandeur. Pole-mounted lights along a walkway assure safety. Motion-detection lights will add to that feeling of safety. Once, these would escalate the power bill. Now such are available in solar-powered form.

Paint the house if you can afford to. Paint the front side of the house if it hasn't been attended to for some time. Even a little paint can go a long way to enhance the curb appeal of a home. Crisp white or light neutral colors selected to blend with the other sides are recommended and colors that can draw the eyes to window treatments will enhance the building's beauty.

The front of your home is the ideal place to invest some sweat equity and recoup big profits during a sale. Better yet, fantastic first impressions will help get a home sold faster and might even attract multiple offers.

While curbside is at the street, remember that you have other exterior spaces that require attention. You have staging to do throughout your yard area. Lawn, trimmed bushes, picnic areas, pool, deck or patio, or a terrace are all features that stand out in the minds of potential buyers and can truly make or break a lucrative deal.

You cannot change the size of the plot of land on which your home rests, but you can certainly enhance what's there. Do it by clearing up and trimming shrubbery, fixing paint and siding, replace worn or cracked pavement, installing privacy fencing. Replace rotted wood and pressure wash (in season) the exterior of your home. Remove all debris from the property. If the jungle gym in your backyard is rusty, ditch it.

Then . . . plant some flowers, put some furniture on the deck and if the weather is suitable, let it with a table setting. Put some candles in outdoor holders, or tiki lamps, if appropriate, particularly if you have an evening showing. If you have a view, arrange your activities to take in the view. Remove all the toys that have accumulated into temporary storage in a garden shed, if available. Curb appeal is relatively easy to maintain in the summer; it's a little more difficult—but no less important—during other parts of the year.

What You're Against

Some people avoid certain homes. Feng shui is a Chinese philosophical system of harmonizing the human existence with the environment. The practice discusses architecture in metaphoric terms of "invisible forces" that bind the Universe, Earth, and man together.

Sell Your Own Home

The goal of feng shui as practiced today is to situate the human built environment on spots with good energy. The "perfect spot" is a location and an axis in time. At http://fengshui.about.com/ you can obtain detail about using the technique for rooms, bedrooms, color, home design, office design, kitchen design, and a host of other applications.

Common Layout Concerns

If you've lived in the home for any length of time, you're accustomed to it. Outsiders may be sensitive to certain issues. Your house may have some of these problems, which will affect the interest of the viewing prospect. You can't change your home, but if these exist, only a person who perceives things as you do will be the candidate to buy your home. It's also true that if these things exist in your home, you have the power to redirect the focus of a buyer's observation:

For the inside stairway facing the entrance: Knowledgeable people hold that this is bad feng shui. Facing a stairway immediately inside a front door is documented to be off-putting. We're not sure why. People seem to like wide, curved, well lit, and positioned at the side. This probably isn't a problem unless you are heir to a mansion or a fan of *Gone With The Wind*.

For the hallway facing the entrance: A buyer wants to enter a home into a warm and inviting front room. Hallways are limiting—a tube that restricts the view. If you happen to own an old brownstone, your home may be designed this way, and possibly, you can't change it. You may have a prospect interested in this form of architecture. Worse, a bathroom at the end of the hallway is singularly uninviting.

Dining room in the center of the house: The dining room becomes a passageway between rooms, and if there is a huge dining table is in the middle, no straight navigation exists around the obstacle.

Adjoining bedrooms are not always considered separate, but should have separate entrances. Long ago, there was a "drawing" room adjacent to the bedroom. For the buyer looking for an older home, this may be acceptable.

People don't buy homes where the living room or dining rooms have doors that lead directly into bedrooms. Noise and privacy are the concerns.

Guest bathrooms accessible by walking through other rooms for access are not good.

Homes that do not appear open, that offer no views from one room to another, will feel small. Open spaces add to the image of sufficient room for a family to operate. Sometimes, opening a wall to an adjacent room can overcome this.

Satellite living rooms are an older feature being revised with family rooms or great-rooms.

Because of the importance of the kitchen for your FSBO activity, this information may be useful. The kitchen is an important room in your house. It is a room packed with energy.

The oven, sink, and refrigerator are called the kitchen triangle. Feng shui aficionados will tell you that this provides balance between the two elements of fire and water.

Continue with good kitchen feng shui colors: Shades of yellow are calming and are good for digestion. Red, brown, and white provide the same balance, whereas blue or black tend to suppress the element of fire.

Clutter and kitchen feng shui require a clutter-free environment, not only of the things you can see, but the things lying willy-nilly inside the cupboards.

Put some fruit or flowers on the kitchen table for good feng shui. Well-displayed utensils, crockery, or cookbooks hold the promise of welcome feelings.

Concentrate on the entrance, kitchen, baths, and master bedroom/suite in your home. You will see results. Make a suitable display of the sight of your home from the street, and invest into cleaning and making an impressive appearance, and the home will become attractive to a potential buyer.

Conclusion

Buyers want to buy a home that has no deferred maintenance, newer appliances, updated plumbing, electrical and heating (including a/c), modern conveniences and is ready to occupy.

Chapter 3

Marketing and Showing Your Home

Marketing Strategies for a Successful Sale

It would be ideal if this business of selling your own home were linear; if the tasks you face could be done one after the other such that once launched you would walk through the process from beginning to end, taking all the appropriate steps along the way.

In the first two chapters of this book, we've covered everything from your motivation to sell to all the steps necessary to prepare your property for sale. From this point on many of these tasks overlap, on the one hand, or must be done concurrently on the other. This chapter will address how and where you should list your property. It will suggest things you can do for yourself and things you must (or should) enlist professionals to assist. It will list many techniques for your consideration, but you should recognize that no one suggestion will do the trick for you. You'll need to experiment. You'll need to try one or more of them.

This is an important point. You began to consider FSBO to save on agent commissions. That's true—it does. Then you were asked to provide an influx of money to the preparation process—repair, landscaping, and the like. If you have been judicious in your selection of improvements, the increases in the selling price of your home have far outdistanced your costs.

Now in this chapter we are going to suggest that you spend more money. It would be easy to assume that you are "nickeled-and-dimed" and the outflow becomes a bit more than you wish to accommodate. Again, your property improvements have cost you money, yes, but that money is recoverable. What those have cost is merely your time and inconvenience. The marketing effort may seem much too much to spend to find and secure a buyer. If your marketing efforts not only achieved a sale price close to your desires but also did it expeditiously, then your investments will have paid off. It costs much more to have the property sit idle, not move, and force you to reduce your price while the situation becomes more pressing and you lose the long-view perspective on a new and better home at a new location.

The marketing of your home must not be a halfhearted effort. If you don't do it right—if you don't do enough of it—you might as well do none of it, and you'll have lost every cent you've paid for it. You cannot recover "sunk" marketing costs. Fail to complete it and you'll be destined to repeat it for as long as you are actively in the market. The FOR SALE BY OWNER sign that remains on your front lawn from now to infinity will require you to reclean, again declutter, and restage your home, probably on only the lead-time of the telephone call of the potential buyer who has called for a viewing. Worse, eventually there will not be any buyers' agents interested in your property because it will have been on the market for too long—and because of that, "something must be wrong with it."

So unless you're willing to drop a thousand bucks to help with the sale of your home, don't even think about doing it. On the other hand, with some investment married to some creativity, you can increase your odds of moving the home quickly, as close to your price as possible. The trick is simple: make yourself unique.

No matter what approach you take, you will be approached by real estate agents who wish exclusively to list your property. In the short term, at least until you have exhausted your FSBO options, resist that action. Once the notification of the offer of your property for sale, it's also more than possible that you will begin to hear from seller's agents. Instead of paying full commission, you may finish paying half commission. Making your property available to selling agents is a wise move for the FSBO seller.

You always have "Self-Marketing" available to you. You can always do all the advertising, conduct all the open house sessions, arrange the buyer visits, and coordinate with the necessary legal requirements. That doesn't change. You always have "Agent Marketing" available to you— list with a realtor.

However, there is a middle ground. You can work with an agent committed to FSBO. The Internet offers FSBO services and ways to solve the issues and arrange the "hoops" you must travel through to see your property sold.

When you have a potential commission cost of $6,000 per $100,000 of the purchase price, it doesn't take long to see that your costs could approach $20,000 quickly on the price of a modern home.

Self-Marketing Tasks

If you choose to do your own marketing, you must do many things; each has an attendant cost. We'll cover those later in the chapter. However, let's simply look at what you would need to do:

- Purchase signs and sign holders and distribute them to appropriate places
- Develop, print, and distribute sales fliers
- Do your own photography

- Develop your own advertising and social media presence
- Hold open houses for each available weekend, as necessary
- Field telephone calls, email and social contacts
- Research and answering questions
- Instigate title searches, appraisals, inspections, escrow, and negotiations
- Develop a contract, normally using a legal forms service
- Work with a Real Estate attorney

The Costs of Self-Marketing

Later in the chapter we'll share why you should use professional looking "for sale" signs. A local sign maker can give accurate costs for your area. You could easily drop a hundred dollars for major signs and somewhat less for directional signs, assuming you can locate legal places to put them.

Advertising isn't cheap, either. You can develop some things with your computer, but professional looking fliers can be pricey, as well. You face Internet advertising, flier advertising, newspaper advertising, and a few others. Display advertising in the paper isn't cheap. Look at the real estate pages in your own newspaper. What's there? Pictures of the street view of the home—important, but limiting. You should avoid classified advertising. It's cheaper, but still restricted, and worse, it doesn't stand apart from the crowd. Advertising and how you do it are crucial. It's the hook at the end of the line, and if you get enough hooks into the water, somebody will bite.

Legal fees are a major concern with self-marketing. They are with any kind of property sale, of course, except that those fees now come from your pocket, not in the settlement on transfer. It is not wise to try to do it without an attorney, and blessedly, in most jurisdictions, it isn't legal, either. If your brother-in-law is an attorney, you might get it for $500. If not, expect to pay at least double that. It's a cost you must absorb.

Listing with a FSBO Service

If your field is advertising, then you have a leg up. If you've done real estate advertising a while, that might be the same. Usually, those of us who put our properties FSBO really haven't the experience to ensure everything that must be done is completed—expeditiously and correctly. Thus using a property-by-owner marketing service is a wise investment. You'll still have to pay the piper, but at least you're dealing with people who can keep you from making major mistakes. Finding one in your area is a veritable plus—and can provide the following services for you:

Signs and riders are a major expense, as mentioned above. You may not be accustomed to obtain a sign with large enough printing or complete enough information for it to be most useful. A rider, by the way, is a second sign, placed above or attached beneath the primary sign, to draw attention to special features or current offers. It might say, "Indoor pool." It might say, "Reduced." It might say, "Offer pending," or it might simply say, "SOLD." That's the one you want, of course.

A FSBO listing service will provide free forms, perform professional photography of your home, write the ad copy, place your property onto Internet websites, create web listings, and provide message service. This becomes a self-service real estate agency for you.

Some FSBO listing services can provide more advertising and exposure than you could do alone. They're established to do so.

Your FSBO service might offer free real estate training.

They'll have the contacts: appraisers, inspections, bank connections, and real estate attorneys.

The Costs of FSBO Listing Services

The service customarily begins at about $200 and tops off at ten times that. You get to choose what services you wish and discuss what variables exist that would allow you join new services or drop old ones. You could easily expend that money, but receive far more for the investment.

It's Time to Be Creative

As a FSBO seller, you want to differ from most real estate agents you'll encounter. You don't have the benefit of on-the-job training, of making mistakes that increase your learning curve. If you want to do that, get some business cards and paint a sign. Place an ad. Wait for the prospects to roll in. No, we're suggesting that you step into the spotlight.

Start by being bold. What can you do to distinguish yourself from every seller of real estate in the area? What might you accomplish if you provided every viewer with information about the area that each can carry away? Think, for a moment, what might happen if you handed out invitations from neighborhood organizations with descriptions of what they offer. What if you obtained and distributed samples of products or handouts from local merchants? It would differ from others.

Next, do things that a realtor might not do. Can you establish a memorable open house activity? Snacks or catering? Activities for the children who accompany an interested buyer?

Your FSBO listing is in your hands. Somebody visits— nobody is expecting you to follow up. Give them a pen with your name and telephone number on it. Give them something magnetic to put on their refrigerator. Find some way to keep your property before their eyes after they have left your home. Give them an incentive to send somebody else to view your home—an insignificant sum, if you will, if they send a buyer your way. Can such an approach work if you produce such a flier for your neighborhood?

The FSBO seller must be different. He must find different ways to ensure people know about his property and enlist them to help. Today, that means using social media. Or it might mean mobile marketing. Or the development of a marketing website.

So what are you afraid of? What stops you from pushing the boundaries in your marketing efforts?

The Marketing Idea

The FSBO idea of marketing is to ensure the home is seen by more people than any other home around. We're interested in proactive techniques that will allow you to take control of your destiny and not wait for a buyer to appear.

Real estate agents have several important jobs. They list the home, put the sign in the yard, show the property to prospective buyers, market to the best of their ability, and handle all the paperwork. The agent handles several properties, either as the seller of your home or as a buyer's agent. She wants to sell a property. The FSBO seller wants to sell his property. If you want your agent to spend all available time promoting your property, then you must be your agent.

Your property is one among hundreds in your area. Unless you do something to make it stand out, it'll be lost, though you've done your best to make it look best and price it for sale.

Social Media and Your FSBO House

Social media is the sound of a clear trumpet that alerts as many homebuyers as you can reach. Finding potential buyers is the hardest part of selling your FSBO property. Anything nontraditional will help.

It's good, but it isn't your first task. That involves finding a realtor who works with FSBO to get your house listed on the MLS® service. That one action will make you available to an army of potential buyers and/or buyer agents.

That creates a foundation for all your social media work. Then tie it to your dedicated website. Ensure contact information is prominently presented.

Once you have the mechanism in place, get the word out, starting with your friends and neighbors. If your life is already involved with social media, now is the time to ask your social networking friends and followers to like, share, or retweet the information. By the time your information has passed through your friends' social media, the word will be out to hundreds; some may pursue interest in your property.

This is important: once you have spread the word, resist bombarding others with it. Overexposure is not good and the social media network in which you're involved will tire of seeing it repeatedly. Keep that effort tied to updates and news. If folks are interested, they'll ask. Seek input— any suggestions? Any advice? Any ideas about how to help me sell this house? Social contacts will rally around you.

Online Curbside Appeal—1234Anystreet.com

Look at the website and you'll find many real estate listings, generally organized according to the real estate agencies in your area. The idea is that when your house's curbside appeal has been established, it's time to broadcast it. The best way to do that is to create your own website to display your property then make a large noise to drive traffic to the home—not the least of which will be a large sign with that URL painted prominently upon it. You can buy a website address for $10 or less for a year, many of which have home page building tools. A key learning point: MLS and any listing agent will put your home on *a* website. You want your home to be on *your* website—a website dedicated exclusively to your property, located here www.1234anystreet.com.

Chances are you are not a website designer. Plenty of people are, and today you can create your own modern-appearing website that will offer your home.

Social Media Positioning

The person who will buy your home is already involved with social media. It is said that more than 90% of homebuyers begin the search on the Internet. He or she has a Facebook page or is present on Twitter, Pinterest, YouTube, or any of several others where the two of you can meet. What will work best for you is to establish on any (or all) of those services a means to find you via your dedicated website. Facebook, for example, will allow you to "promote" your "status" for a low fee, with the ability to target a specific geographic location. Facebook has recently passed through a billion users—and many of those are within your area. Some of those are looking for your FSBO notification. Overexposure here is not a problem. However, make sure you have designated your posting "public." That way, anybody with an interest in FSBO homes will be able to find you.

Except somebody moving from a significant distance, anybody who finds your dedicated website has a complete understanding of the "from/to" aspects of your advertisement. He or she knows where the desirable areas of the region are and if you're located there, anybody with that knowledge will pursue you. Add the selling price to your link and you'll narrow the number of people who click merely to learn how much the house sells for. The process is called "pay-per-click," and you are charged a connection fee for anybody who will consider the possibility of the purchase of your home. Charges will vary over service and over time, of course, but a cost of 35 to 50 cents is customary. You can't market much more inexpensively than that. Put a call to action on your ad. New users to Facebook and Google Plus hosting plans obtain credits to be applied to those charges. Pictures posted on Pinterest or Instagram can provide a survey to your potential buyer. Virtual tours conducted on YouTube allow you to lead them through the property, emphasizing the things you feel are important.

Today few telephone books exist. The Smartphone can locate nearly everything you need. The information generation has an obsession to connectivity. They're online everywhere, all the time, even those shopping for a new home. Therefore, make sure, when somebody finds you, your website contains current and relevant information. What should be on your website? How about your listing document? This list contains lots of information about your property and you should present it as a clean, well-presented list:

- The address
- The municipality or neighborhood
- The school district
- Price of the house
- When the house was built
- How many rooms
- How many bedrooms and bathrooms
- Approximate dimension of the rooms
- Recent upgrades and improvements
- The features of the location
- Photos, photos, photos

Include a narrative that emphasizes the best and most appealing features of the home. Include also well-lit and uncluttered pictures from several angles of the rooms, including the kitchen and living room. You would be wise to hire a professional photographer, but it is possible to do it yourself. Also, strongly consider the virtual tour.

Close in usage is the social media service known as Twitter. In Twitter, people communicate (140 characters or fewer), expressing their interests, reactions, and real-time information. It has been said that half-a-billion users spend to three hours per month glued to that one service alone. You don't have to say much on Twitter— use it as a teaser and create a link to your dedicated website. It will also allow you to interact, briefly, with anyone to respond to questions.

Sell Your Own Home

Like Facebook, Twitter is free and easy to use. It's an outstanding way to give your listing more links. One thing that you can do on Twitter is to make your listing "retweetable." You can set it up for your readers to share it forward. Once you have a list of people who have an interest to buy, or friends of friends interested, you can make perpetual changes to that 140 characters (be sure to include a small picture), and they will be spread abroad. One of the fun things about using Twitter is that you will learn some abbreviations used by realtors, such as *ba* (bathroom), *br* (bedroom), *ofc* (home office), *hdwd* (hardwood floors), etc. There is a whole jargon used in what we'll call "compressed advertising," i.e., the newspaper classifieds and, of course, Twitter.

Another good feature of Twitter is the hashtag. Hashtags are grouping mechanisms used on social media. Hashtags like #FSBO, #forsalebyowner, and #homesforsale can be used to place your listing in a way it is searchable via Twitter.

Instagram and Pinterest also provide news ways to promote the property you wish to market. More people than ever are using the Internet to review the available homes in the area. To use either, you'll need high-quality photographs. These photos must be taken with high quality photographic equipment, and unless you are prepared to hire that service, you should learn how to take such photos. Good-quality cell phone photos are useful, but only the best should be uploaded to Instagram and Pinterest.

Instagram users have also the opportunity to locate you on a map, but be sure to tag your photo when you submit it. This is the perfect way to connect with potential buyers in your geographic area, and if not them, then someone they know.

Tying your Twitter, Facebook, Pinterest, and Instagram accounts together allows you to post current information on all (that are linked) with the smallest effort. The advantage of this is obvious: less work. The hidden advantage is that it opens your information to hundreds of others who seek what you offer. Keep it simple. Use it to get people to go to your dedicated website. Offer incentives for others to spread the word.

YouTube is unique. With little effort, and using other sites that will help you to post to YouTube, you can upload virtual tours and obtain the maximum return for your efforts. A video makes a powerful statement. When something "goes viral," chances are it's available to more than a billion people, not all who will call you, of course. YouTube conveys key information. It allows you to create short, informative, and comprehensive views of what you have to offer. It takes a little effort to get it started, but it is an extraordinary way to present your home to the world.

You want to reach your maximum audience. Traditional methods still work, and we're about to give information about them. If you really want to sell your home quickly, chances are high that the social media will provide the quickest actual response and return for your money.

Social media costs aren't significant, no matter the options selected. Craigslist, for example, is free for the using. There are other lists on which you can put alluring pictures of your property and links to your dedicated website. You don't have to go directly to the social website to do it. The services of Photobucket will do it for you.

Sell Your Own Home

One thing we know about social media. The modern property buyer is there and is looking. After your listings have been placed, take time each day to update the story, to tell something about your home that may "snag" the interest of a homebuyer. Once it is known, it will develop a following, and one day you will make the appropriate comment that drives the viewer to your website. Think for a minute what might happen if you ran a little contest about painting a kitchen (yellows and soft shades of red, by the way). People will follow as you update your status each step along the way. Keep it fresh and keep it moving. Followers will follow.

It works. The more people you get to look at your home—first online—and subsequently in person—the greater the possibility you have to move the property. All you have to do is to create accounts with the various social media services.

Using Social Media to Find Your Ideal Buyer

The Internet has given consumers extraordinary power for searching out a new home. Because of that, FSBO sellers wishing to present their homes to a wide and diverse audience have outstanding opportunities.

The key is strategy. Social media represents a selection of digital platforms and tools awaiting content. That content is your home. Bring your property to notice of everybody imaginable. Not only are billboard and bus benches available, you now can add videos of your home to your website, giving virtual tours. Clients can now be comfortable—and not under any pressure—while they view your home. When they actually show up at your front door to see the real thing, you can be assured that what they saw online they liked. Because of that, they are ready to buy. That is smart social media marketing.

Social media marketing is dynamic. You can update your status and tweet out new bits of information throughout the day. You can develop your material and have it automatically appear at the various venues you have established. Once you have begun, you have an outstanding opportunity to talk to anyone who views, using a "blog." Using your blog, you can share your properties and tell why they are important to you. When you do that, you introduce yourself to a prospect. He or she determines whether to do business with you and, perhaps, to hear a greater story—first hand—about the property you offer. Add a comment section to your blog and the interaction permits you to size each other up. Then, when you show your property to the prospect, you'll have a solid idea of the other's interests and concerns.

Please—from this point on, no amateur photography. Yes, you can certainly take pictures. Are you adept enough to ensure the best possible angle is considered, that lighting is perfect, that the staging will fit the picture? If you want to do a video walk-through, do you even have the equipment that will permit you to do that? Think about old videos you might have shot. Were they shaky? Was the light bad? Did you cut people's heads off the picture? You need to spend the money to get a decent set of pictures and possibly a video that will present your property in the best possible way.

Because you have provided the buyer with a mechanism to evaluate the property and you, they will come prepared to deal. Again, the more you can present about your home, the better able you'll be to attract a buyer who has a sincere interest. Further, done properly, social media will allow you to keep in touch with interested parties from anywhere.

The Advantages of Internet Advertising

The idea of advertising, of course, is to move your property quickly. It's better yet if you can do so inexpensively. Many ways exist to get the word out. The Internet is among the best, for the following reasons:

- Broad exposure than other media
- Full-time message presentation
- The ability to measure the effectiveness of your advertisements
- You can target your ad specifically to the interested segment
- Costs are limited to people who have a specific interest in your property
- Insertion costs are not repeating costs
- You aren't committed to a specific message; you can change it as needed

People today start looking on the Internet. Be there.

Social Media as Leverage for Home Presentation

When you decide to put your home on the market and use social media to promote it, then it follows that you can conduct your open house there, as well. Of course, you can use it for your announcement, but if you think about it, you can actually conduct a part of your open house there. Pictures make a difference. The narrative that follows those pictures and fed to your social media in dibs and dabs create anticipation and expectation. Put directions to the physical open house, attach a property flier, extend the invitation, see who has sent RSVPs, and use it to send reminders. Put it on your Facebook wall and ask your friends to spread it.

Lawn Signs

Though it predates social media, the sign on the front lawn of your property continues to have great use. While not necessarily used by every home seller, they are an absolute must for the FSBO seller. Many people buy houses that they see while out for a drive in a neighborhood of interest. While you can certainly make your own sign, a professionally prepared sign can make a gigantic difference. A bad sign might cause the viewer to wonder about the conditions inside the home. A worthy sign projects that you are professional and prepared. People will judge you by the sign you display. A good sign causes an evaluation of the curb appeal and leads the viewer to assume that the inside is of the same quality.

Remember, you may never know where your buyer became aware of your property. He may indeed find it on the Internet, but there's also the possibility that he's responding to a newspaper advertisement or the recommendation of someone aware of your home—friend or neighbor. He simply drives past your home. You want that person to know what you offer.

The sign in the front of your home is working around the clock (though better in the daylight). Many people who view your sign will not have engaged a realtor yet.

Is it a substitute for other methods of advertising, particularly social media? No. However, the statistics tell us that ten to twenty percent of the FSBO calls you receive are based on the sign stuck into the front lawn. Certainly if your home is on a thoroughfare, having a sizable and attractive sign is an absolute plus. It is of less value on a short side street or in a cul-de-sac, of course, but is still a worthwhile asset. Directional signs, at every change of direction, will lead viewers to your property.

Where to buy a sign? Some sign makers are within your reach. You can also buy signs online reasonably. Have them customized with what you want on the sign and shipped right to your door!

What should that yard sign convey? It should certainly convey the Internet address that leads them to your website. It should also present a telephone number where you can be reached. Does it have to say FSBO? Wouldn't hurt, because the potential buyer will know that the price may be more reasonable than if an agent is involved. If you choose to include the asking price, that will cull the nuisance calls made simply to determine the price. While it is certainly your choice, it is recommended that you do include the price. You are not a real estate agent. You have a singular goal: sell *your* house. A real estate agency is content to sell *a* house. Put the price there and anybody qualified to buy your house and interested to view your house will call you, thereby eliminating the option for the agent to steer a client in a different, and more lucrative (to the realtor) property.

You might also consider a statement that says the showing is done by appointment. Most important, and in larger type, the phone number and Internet address. Stay away from too many items on a sign; stick to the most important items. One important item that may seem optional is to notify the sign reader that a certified appraisal is available. More on that later in the chapter.

A FSBO yard sign is a frame, a printed panel, and a brochure dispenser. In that brochure dispenser will go printed sheet or a trifold that will extol the features of the house and the unique things the property offers. A Good-quality dispenser will keep your literature dry and protected from the elements, allowing the drive-by audience the ability to take the pertinent information with you. In a day when computers are ubiquitous, you can produce your own information sheets and even trifold brochures. Involve yourself with an agent who handles FSBO signs.

Size matters, and the larger the better, but the sign need not be gigantic. A sign size of 18" x 24" should be sufficient, but raise that half again if necessary. No need to paint a sheet of plywood. You can get signs and sign holders that will complement the landscaping. However, lettering size on that sign matters much. Your buyer needs to view it without stopping, moving at least within the neighborhood speed limit.

Where should it be located and how should it be positioned? In the simplest of terms, at right angles to the street. This affords a "cruiser" sufficient time to take the contents of the sign in visually. If you put it parallel to the house, the passengers will either have to stop to read it or crane their necks to see. For obstructions, such as shrubbery, lawn ornaments, or other buildings along the street, you need to position the sign for the clearest view. Once you decide where to put it, get out and drive around the block and see for yourself how it appears.

Obtain sign materials that permit add-ons—extra signs stood upright at the top or hanging from rings at the bottom. This will permit you to highlight features on smaller signs that you can change periodically. It will allow you to announce events, such as an open house.

You may be fortunate and sell your home within days of posting your sign. Some do. More often, the sign may stay in your yard for a longer period. This means that a flimsy cardboard sign or even a more durable plastic sign is insufficient. Signs are moved about in the wind. They are beaten upon by hot sun and precipitation, often including extremes of temperature. They must be substantial to be durable enough to last through the exercise.

In summary: there is no point to have a great sign if people cannot see it. Make it attractive, durable, and useful to your purpose.

Newspaper Classifieds

Look at the classifieds that accompany your next "real estate" day distribution of your local newspaper. You'll find many FSBO ads there and become aware that everybody who placed them was attempting to garner hundreds of thousands while spending few nickels to place them. Make certain that you establish a marketing budget and stick by it.

Classified advertising can be expensive, but if you're smart, that advertising will give you great exposure and great opportunity. How do you know that people scrimp on the ads? Look at the abbreviations the ads include. You need to evaluate alternatives and compare costs. Be on the lookout for multiday specials or specific times of the month that offer better deals. Over time, watch to see if the medium offers specials and whether there are additional charges for carrying pictures. You would be wise to schedule your advertisements when you plan open house sessions; otherwise, you'll be doing things one at a time. Here's a sneaky idea: watch for when other properties in your neighborhood plan to conduct open house sessions. Set yours for the same time and you'll get the benefit of people in your area anyway.

The question is whether your ad should include every detail you can cram into a column inch. You've decided that the best deal for your pocketbook would be to do it by the month, and that's good. The house may sell within a month, but you'd better plan on two or three. Present the teaser—strictly the teaser—as if you were writing a Twitter ad. Put a small picture with a price and a website address. Unless there is something unusual—a pool, perhaps—don't try to use the classifieds to sell your home. Use them to whet the appetite with only enough information to cause them to call you.

In your ad, be sure always to include the neighborhood, the address, or at least the proximity to some major landmark. Tell the number of bedrooms and baths. Give the square footage. Tell the reader about the garage and anything unusual about the house. If the house was recently built, give its age. Tell of upgrades: furnace, air-conditioning, sprinkling fields, swimming pool, hot tub, size of garden, or whatever you have that will draw a prospect's interest.

It's a cliché, but appropriate: "Sell the sizzle, not the steak." You ad must make the home desirable. It must not be merely a recitation of the facts.

While proximity to a good school system or public transportation is important, keep that information from your advertisement. You don't want to hold any buyer at arm's length, and that kind of information might do that. Convey no messages of desperation. If the buyer sees "motivated seller" in the ad, expect a low bid.

If it's an open house ad, the address is necessary. If you have received a certified house appraisal, say so. Be sure to include your website and your telephone number. Again, you want to sell *your* house, not merely *a* house.

Effective Advertisements

FSBO sellers must advertise. Those advertisements require some effort. These are the major tasks of the advertisements, either in the newspaper or on the Internet:

- Write an attention-getting headline. "For Sale by Owner" is "plain vanilla." Something like "The Best Home Purchase Value" might be more effective.
- Provide a clear benefit that will give the advertising reader a reason to continue. "Move-In Condition; Major Appliances Included,"
- Include a call to action. You're looking to inspire somebody's action and you must do it with an action of your own: "Join us Saturday morning [date] for coffee and cookies." Don't offer a financial incentive if you haven't thought it completely through.

Here's an example:

> *Horse property: A Modern Stainless Kitchen and Paneled Family Room! If you're looking for a 4 bedroom, 2 bath, in the Plumburg Neighborhood, this split-level ranch with a fully finished basement on ¾ acre horse property is yours for $435,000. Seller is willing to hold a second mortgage. You can take a visual tour at 1234Anystreet.com or call us at 800-555-1212 for an exciting experience. Bring your horse for a ride in our spacious arena.*

Now that the advertisements have been written to attract the readers' attention and persuades them to take action, you'll need to find the best places to post them. Post your ads online, in the newspaper, with alternative weekly editions, and on all the local directories you can find.

Selling your house FSBO requires that you do all the work that a realtor would. However, if you want to save some money and are ready to do all the work yourself, these FSBO home-selling tips will definitely help you advertise effectively! As you develop the information to publicize, you'll be interested in:

- Construction: Frame or brick or some combination or both; masonry, stone, or stucco.
- Condition: Remodeled, recently decorated, immaculate, restored, one owner, year built
- Basement Features: Finished, open, cedar closet, recreation room, workshop
- Financing: Assumption possible, owner second, low rate, submit offer
- Land: Acreage, lot size, fenced, landscaped, sprinkler, barn and horse facilities, trees, waterfront, ravine
- Interior Specifics: Rooms, bedrooms, bathrooms, fireplaces, square footage
- Location: Schools, shopping, transportation, neighborhood features, tennis courts, golf course, park, on a cul-de-sac.

Fliers

Once you have gathered all the information you wish to publish about your home, you might consider preparing fliers. These fliers will be stored in a document box on your sign. As you prepare to hold an open house (discussed in a later chapter) you will wish to flood your neighborhood with fliers and perhaps even "paper" a local parking lot with them. Fliers are also effective on community bulletin boards.

The flier you want is 8.5" x 11", standard for the North American Continent. Other parts of the world use A4 paper, slightly smaller. The flier will present relevant facts that you are willing to divulge to the prospect. They are the "carry away" from your sign or your open house. Don't tell the whole story—keep some of it a mystery for the viewer to solve—but put yourself in the buyer's shoes to anticipate property details you would want to know.

Pick a headline. The headline captures the reader's attention. What is the property's strongest feature? Something like: "The Safest Neighborhood in the City."

Sell the dream that will capture the imagination of your prospect. The buyer will want details, yes, but the flier should provide only the level of detail that will trigger contact. Something like: "Luxury Living at a Budget Price."

This flier is not the great novel you will one day produce. You must tell the story of your home in a brief paragraph, highlighting features that might attract buyers. What is unique about your property? How does your property differ from others? Keep it simple, but build upon the emotions that your home can produce—the view, the neighborhood, the gardening space, the flowerbeds, etc.

Insert pictures—certainly of the exterior, to remind the curious what the home looks like from the outside, and if you have room on the flier for several smaller pictures, tell a brief story about the inside of the house. Use the backside of the paper. Your flier can be a two-surface canvas.

Provide insight about how you loved the property and paid attention to the details. Tell them about the construction, condition, flooring, size, bedrooms, bathrooms, information about the basement, and some description of the land.

Tell them how to contact you: phone number, website, and appointment requirements.

Do not put it on copy paper. Obtain glossy finished paper and make it look professional. Put some in a weatherproof box on the kitchen counter or by the front door when you show the home.

Making a flier isn't difficult. If you have the computer skills, you can take the photos you've prepared, position them on the paper, and fill the open spaces with the appropriate text that makes your effort inviting. If you do not have the skills, online services are available for little money that will help preparation of the flier and then print them for you. Free help is available on the Internet. Enter "sales flier templates" into Google.

Some Advice about Taking Pictures

Before the days of Internet advertising, the first exposure of a FSBO home was either an article in the newspaper or the drive-by, done by prospects. Today it's different. You'll have lookers on your website first. They may decide whether they're interested before they venture out to your open house. Remember the importance of a first impression. Take extraordinary effort on the photo shoot. Plan well beforehand.

Then, their first physical impression is the curb appeal of your home. You've gone to the trouble to make the outside of your home outstanding. Now capture that look in your camera and post those pictures online. Or hire a professional to do so.

You then will post them on your social media pages or in your advertisements, and that's what they either see directly or which is sent to them via e-mail from a seller's agent. Photos must reflect well on the property.

You must have high-resolution photos. Smartphone camera pictures will be fine between you and your friends, but that's not sufficient for publicity. Put an experienced photographer with a quality camera to work. You must have those photos before you ever put your home FSBO. Put up a listing without a picture and potential buyers will pass right over it and may never return.

Photo shoots should happen when the home has the best natural light. The house must be fully cleaned and at least decluttered. Stage the pictures as you can. Your home is now a product for sale and the pictures are the marketing campaign designed to attract prospects.

Picture this: by whatever method, the prospective buyer has found you and your home. He learns that you have a website on with an exhaustive set of high quality pictures. Once he is interested, he will arrange to meet an open house or arrange a showing. He now walks through your home, recognizing room after room that he saw in your picture gallery. He thanks you and leaves then goes home with your property on his mind. Now he calls out the listing on the Internet, and again views those pictures, returning repeatedly to compare your home to others he has viewed. The more he looks through the gallery of pictures of your home, the more he begins to identify himself in that space. He then begins to expound to his spouse on the values of what you offer. Your pictures will convert him from an interested observer to a salesman on your behalf. Here's the process:

If you choose to prepare the photographs yourself, use a tripod. It lessens the shakiness.

Prepare the property for the photo shoot. Mow your lawn, trim the bushes, and clear all the clutter from the yard.

Take your indoor shots after cleaning everything inside the house. You will want to do so before you stage it anyway. If you have strobe lights, they will brighten the dark spots. Do not close the blinds and curtains and turn the lights on. It gives you a halo around the lamp. Use natural light, but don't shoot sunlight streaming through the windows. Whenever you take the picture, use the flash on the camera to even things out.

Take photos with the furniture cut a minimum and arranged attractively. This shows the room as it is lived-in. However, you might be wise not to show your life-worn furniture. Don't run out and buy new furniture, but you might consider renting modern and new furniture temporarily. Pay attention to the details. Balance the room—overstuffed chairs, couches, ottomans, etc. For eating surfaces, space the chairs evenly and uniformly.

Photograph the outside of the home from the street in wide shots from several angles. Then do the same from the back. Good selling points will include garages, shops, porches, athletic courts, water fountains, garden, etc.

Your kitchen has a style that you must capture in your pictures. Viewers want to see the cabinets, counter-tops, appliances, island or food preparation areas, and any dinette facilities.

Your living room, family room, or den must be captured from all angles. What's unique about the room?

Fireplaces, window treatment, shelving, screens, and even ceiling fans might be photographed.

Make the beds with color. Remove the clutter. Take photos from every angle that demonstrates light and space, including closets. If you have walk-in closets, try to show their sizes in the photo.

Put out your prettiest towels and bathmats when you take photos of all the bathrooms. Include all the fixtures and cabinets in the pictures.

Somebody is going to want to see the garage and the basement. Make it as neat as possible. By now, you have decluttered both.

Exterior shots of brick and concrete will appear bright. If you wash them down before taking the picture, the brick color will stand out and the gloss of finished concrete will be dulled. Similarly, if you have a pool, take your picture on a cloudy day or late in the afternoon after the glare of the sun is gone.

Again, consider hiring a professional. You're competing against people who have. Photos matter. A professional can tell a story of what it's like to live in the home. The idea of the pictures, after all, is to sell the house. Nevertheless, if you insist on taking your own pictures, here's what you need to know:

Use a Good-quality digital camera from which you can upload pictures to your computer. Select a camera that gives you the ability to take low light, wide-angle pictures. A wide-angle lens allows you to move closer to the building to obtain a complete shot that may remove items from the foreground. Since you intend to use this camera inside the house, obtain one to which you can attach an external flash.

When your home is staged, put the camera on a tripod and establish the shot in the viewfinder. On the exterior, take the picture without the car in the driveway and with the garage door closed. Include NO yard toys, recycle or trash bins, or even your FSBO sign. Before you close the shutter, ensure the vertical lines appear vertical in the viewfinder. If they do not, you are probably experiencing "barrel distortion." Move further away from the vertical line and stand slightly to either side. Obviously, take pictures of the outstanding features.

Inside photography is a little different. Here you want natural light, but not the bright sunshine. Better to do it on a bright but slightly overcast day. Be careful when photographing diagonals, as digital pictures can create a slightly jagged picture. Again, use the tripod. No shaky pictures. Shoot reflective surfaces at an angle to minimize light bounce back to the camera.

Some Oddities

Consider having magnetic signs prepared for the sides of your vehicle or on the back door or trunk. Picture this:

4BR/2BA ON 3 ACRES
[NEIGHBORHOOD]
MODERN KITCHEN
PHONE NUMBER
WEB: 1234STREET.COM

Or a sign that says simply: GOOGLE: 1234 STREET. Get your property website on the Internet and all a passerby must remember is the address. The message is simple as it can be. This is your billboard advertising at a red light or parked on the street or in a lot. It will draw.

Sell Your Own Home

If you have decided to allow a buyer's agent to approach your FSBO, you can help your cause with a little positive effort. If you have time to observe, note all the properties in your area for at least two months, more if you can. Take note of the realtor with whom they are listed. When that listing disappears from the paper, write that realtor a letter explaining that you intend to FSBO, but that you will welcome an approach by a seller's agent. You'll be splitting the commission, but it will help move the property. Be creative: one seller is known to have written the letter on behalf of the property.

If you are a real estate speculator, chances are you can help a buyer. The message that you can carry the note or at least a note for a down payment for a prospect who can handle the mortgage but can't qualify for the entire loan will bring some of those forward. You will need to be cautious on the financials, but failing a different approach, you might try it. Seller financing can increase the size of the buyer group.

Rent a window. If you have a street-level downtown store or office or can purchase the space briefly, develop a picture show of your home and present it using a digital picture frame. It looks modern. Find a way to include your printed listing, and that may draw some folks to an open house. You can use a service called Animoto to develop your show—which can be the same show you load up to YouTube or your website.

One thing you will begin to see is mobile marketing. This is the Smartphone generation. You will find services that will notify people about your home as they drive by.

However you present your property, remember also that marketing is what brings people who look, while pricing is what obtains buyers.

The Certified House Appraisal

Consider a sign that looks like this:

4BR/2BA ON 3 ACRES
[NEIGHBORHOOD]
CERTIFIED APPRAISAL AVAILABLE
PHONE NUMBER
WEB: 1234STREET.COM

The greatest task a FSBO seller has is determining what to ask for the home he or she is selling. Certainly, a seller wants the best possible price for the property. As certain is the fact that the buyer wants value for the money spent. To sell the house you will have to obtain—and pay for—several inspections. One often requested by a financial institution will be the Certified House Appraisal, or CHA. You may sell the property for more, particularly in a bidding situation. You may sell the property for less for myriad reasons. A CHA, however, will shortstop the abundance of "low bid tests" you will encounter. It is testimony—certified testimony—as to the actual value of your home on the local market at the time the snapshot is taken.

A CHA is one method to overcome a buyer's reluctance. Initially, it's the fear that they will offer too much for the home. This differs from an appraisal for property taxes. A close-by fear is whether prospects can afford the home—i.e., can they handle the mortgage payment? By now, the savvy buyer has learned that if he gets a commitment from a lender before he starts to look for a home, and if he is realistic in what he can spend beyond that financing, the ability to match it to a CHA becomes a positive step.

Sell Your Own Home

A buyer may know the house has been available for some time—what they might consider too much time. You and I know that the house has been searching for a realistic and acceptable price—often because of a sense of intrinsic worth not supported by the facts. The prospect, on the other hand, is too polite to ask, but is actually thinking, "What's wrong with it?"

A third fear is one of commitment—not to a mortgage, but to personal stability. If the buyer needs a house but is unsure whether employment will be stable, then there is a natural reluctance to obtain something that might be difficult to resell should the need arise. He or she may be in the mental mindset of waiting for more personal stability. The answer is to emphasize the resale ability of the property and tell about about financial options that will help the resale.

Another fear is the natural caution about being "ripped off." 'Who do you trust' is a game that every homebuyer plays. A home is the major investment in a family's life and many people are involved: you, the FSBO seller, potentially a buyer's agent, lenders, builders, perhaps, movers, financial agencies, consultants, lawyers. Everybody involved is in for a piece of the action. It's a natural fear to handle when you're not certain that you will be treated fairly by everyone. You can do reference checks. You can verify claims with the Better Business Bureau. You can check ethics panels for the professionals involved. Your best business strategy determines what you can afford then get what you want in a home.

When you're asked how you established a price, you can hand over your CHA and suggest that the prospect look it through. The existence of a certification removes the incidents of contest over the reasonableness of the price. That report establishes credibility; leave it out for anyone to see during the open house. Highlight the appraisal value. It will eliminate low offers and it can help your buyer to finance, should the lending agency question the property's value. When you seek a Certified House Appraiser, be sure to identify the banks and lending institutions that accept his appraisals for mortgages. No doubt, it will match the buyer's lender, but if not, you can recommend the alternate financing source. The cost of obtaining the appraisal is an investment in your property that can ultimately pay thousands.

The format of the appraisal is uniform. It should include photos of the outside of the home and any outbuildings, with narrative descriptions that tell how the value was derived.

Initially, it will compare your property to similar properties. It will detail the current costs to build the homes per square foot then added improvements that "live" with the property—air-conditioning, sprinkling systems, fireplace, redevelopment, and any other items that would not travel with you when you leave. From this, there will be adjustments, both positive and negative, for wear and refurbishing.

From this analysis, you will have the market value (as the home exists) and a cost value with adjustments brought on by renovations. The market value will be of interest to the buyer and his financier. Of course, that assumes that the seller is willing to accept the appraiser's market value. If not, any agreed -upon price between the seller and a buyer becomes the market value of the transaction. However, that doesn't change the true market value. If the buyer is unwilling to accept a higher number, the home goes back on the market while its price gradually accedes to the true market value or below.

The cost approach has value, as well. Highlight it and draw to the buyer's attention that the larger figure is an estimate of real value beyond the requested selling price.

A logical question, having spent so much time discussing using the Internet, is why not obtain an appraisal via an online service? It's a cheap service, and you get what you pay for. However, here is not where you need to save money. Ever encountered a Google Earth, a service that gives street views? If so, you can understand that it would be easy to estimate based on the picture. You will have provided details of the property and these services have access to property data from public sources. The online activity does an "armchair" assessment and speaks in generalities. You want $350,000 for your home, perhaps, and the online assessment pegs it within a range starting at $320,000 and extended above your price. You may have said you want to sell for $375,000, recognizing that you will come down to $350,000, but the buyer has the low value of $320,000 in mind and he'll not budge far from that.

On the other hand, a certified house appraisal, done by a local appraiser, carries weight with a financial institution. The price for your home is established, and the credibility carries assurance that all parties are treated fairly.

Now that we've taken care of getting out the word, the result we expect is that your phone and/or your doorbell begin(s) to ring. The next step is to show your home.

Ken Lord

Showing Your House

The Open House Philosophy

Few open houses result in the immediate offer of a purchase agreement. You should understand that. Most will attract many for whom the open house is a Sunday activity. Some will attract neighbors who are simply curious. If your house had been listed with an agent, he or she might have agreed to a single showing, without you present, and would have been as interested in obtaining another listing as in showing yours.

The chances are that if you have prepared an Internet presence and conducted a virtual tour, many people who show up might have already taken that tour and now wish to match the real thing to the video, if for no other reason than to ensure you're on the up-and-up.

For this section, however, you should assume that people who show up at your door are serious prospects. Your role now is to convert them into "offerors," from which you will obtain at least one buyer.

To do this, you must stage a scene where potential buyers can picture themselves. You need to draw them into your picture and make them feel at home. The dilemma you face here is that you want your home to feel cozy and welcoming to everyone while creating the impression that it can belong to only one person, couple, or family. Thus, cliché though it is, you have only one chances to make a dramatic and lasting impression.

Think about that for a moment. Yes, you have a sign on the lawn and you have signs directing the driver at every step from the thoroughfare. If you prospect pulls up in front of your home and discovers an unkempt yard—grass that needs to be cut, bushes that need to be trimmed, weeds that need to be pulled—he's going to put the car into gear and go on to the next open house. Nobody in his right mind will purposely subject himself to what appears to be much recovery work. He might be accepting of the periodic maintenance to keep it looking good, but if it doesn't look good to begin with, you'll probably not see him at your entrance.

It's obvious that you must make the outside look inviting. Realtors call that "curb appeal." Mowing the lawn, trimming the bushes, and pulling the weeds aren't all, however. How would you react if there were a front porch and on that porch was a welcoming rocking chair? Could you picture yourself there, rocking, watching the world go by?

Suppose the door had been painted a bright red? Would you wish to enter? Whatever the color, a fresh coat of paint on the door makes it look inviting. Suppose nothing metal in the front yard had any rust—light fixtures, mailboxes, or house number? Suppose the house has a street number that can be seen from the street? Would that be attractive to you?

Now suppose the buyer, his wife, and two children show up at the door and because you have a welcome, walk-in sign, they open the door and enter. What will they see? You know that the idea is for you to move and because of that, you've begun your packing for the sole purpose of reducing clutter. Will your prospect enjoy the additional space? Yes, anybody who buys your house is certain to clutter it up again, but what will be the impact when they see that your home is clean and need—and presentable.

A family wants to envision itself within the bounds of the home they are viewing. Will they be pleased that

Junior's athletic trophies are packed away, that the family photos you had there until yesterday are removed, and that your daughter's room has now been painted a pleasant but neutral color. The "Princess" motif has now been removed, and that makes the viewing family happy because their "princess" has now outgrown Disney.

As the prospects walk through the house, what do you think their perspectives are that you have retained only the things required for day-to-day living? They know you had such things, as they do now, but they look, and the boxes in which you have certainly packed such things have been removed to storage facilities. Can you feel the gratitude for the ability to move easily around the home, examining storage spaces and opening closets?

Mrs. Open House Viewer is taken with the neatness of the kitchen and the colors of the towels that decorate the bathrooms. She wonders how she would keep the bedrooms looking so spacious and well appointed. Because the closets are only partially used, she can envision the space as something she wishes to emulate in the new home. She doesn't need to know that you had to donate half your wardrobe to the Rescue Mission to make it look that way.

Mr. Open House Viewer is more interested in the basement and the garage. He's had a chance to envision how his woodshop equipment will fit. He sees that tool storage space in the basement and yard equipment storage space is large enough to accommodate his own supply, with room left over. He doesn't have to know that you've taken every spare rake and shovel and every out-of-season yard tool and put them in storage to make it look that way.

Sell Your Own Home

You kept only enough furniture in each room to show the room's purpose, exposing all the wall space you can and removing the ottomans, coffee tables, extra chairs, and TV trays that seem to occupy so much space. You had a little time, so you painted the room. You read somewhere that coating the walls with neutral colors makes the rooms look larger. It's true. It's amazing how bright and breezy the rooms now seem. The family room is nice, but over the years, it became a cave. Once you've pulled the extra furniture and refreshed the wall color, your visitor can picture her brood there.

There were a few things you had to remember to do. During the day, you kept the drapes open; at night, they were closed and the room's lighting was used. Now that the "cave" is gone, you found it easier to maintain the room. Daily cleaning there became easy. You've could keep the entire home swept, mopped, dusted, and vacuumed in far less time than you used to take. You'll need to remember how you did that in your new home.

The viewing family may not say so, but they fully appreciate that the absence of dishes in the sink, the beds are made, the laundry is collected somewhere near the location of the washing machine. They appreciate that the house is in showroom condition. Now the idea is to play a little soothing music and to ensure no pets are in the home.

A final word about the open house philosophy: people don't want to walk through a home when your entire family is there. She may wish to stay with the house while he may take the kids for a ride. A wiser move would be to park the kids with grandma for the day and show the house as a couple. This will certainly provide more protection than with one person alone. More than that, someone will be available to answer any question.

After The Decision is Made

You've decided to offer your home FSBO. You've taken all the steps to declutter, clean, and stage your house. If the house is sold on the day after, you're golden. Chances are the process can take a month, or two—or even three. You know that within a few weeks you're going to have to open the house for strangers to walk through. You'll need a plan to protect your valuables, yet. Already you're receiving calls from agents wanting to list your property (they found your advertising or drove by your house). If you haven't yet, you'll be receiving inquiries from buyers' agents wanting to know if they can show your home. If you've decided you are willing to entertain the "half commission" route, then you'll need to sign some forms, give the agent a walk-through before he or she produces a client, and... horrors! You'll have to clean the place again!

Of course, once you have done your thorough cleaning and staging, it's simple to keep it ready for multiple showings, right? Wrong! If you intend to leave the home staged and move out before the house is sold, then perhaps that will work. More realistically, between the time you've decided to sell and the actual showing(s), you'll probably live in the house—which means more meals, more laundry, more newspapers and magazines and other forms of clutter.

None of us has found a way to clean a home, live in it, and keep it pristine. Yours will not be the first. Nor will the Merry Maids pop in each day to "bring the place up to snuff." Do you need some guidance on how to keep the house up, especially since your family is accustomed to doing anything but help? If you believe the information at www.FlyLady.net, you can do the whole job in about 20 minutes per day. The website is a good source of cleaning information, but you might not wish to become nervous over a cleaning regimen. The premise is that if you adopt some ritual cleaning habits, the need to apply special efforts and substantial time to crisis cleaning (someone is on the way over) will subside.

Have a keep-it-clean plan for open houses. With a plan of attack, you can keep your home presentable with minimum daily efforts. At the least, it will keep your home appearing "showroom fresh," such that final adjustments can be made between the time you receive a call and a prospect arrives.

Start at the kitchen. If your kitchen is like many, it's the gathering point for the family, where communication occurs. Keep the sink spotless; load the dishwasher as quickly as you have rinsed off the dishes. Wipe the countertops, range and refrigerator contact points. Give the floor a once-over.

Go next to the bathroom. Become accustomed to wiping the sink when you wash your hands, clean your teeth, or remove your makeup. Use a premoistened wipe around the edges of the sink, the tub (or shower door) and the exposed porcelain anywhere in the room. Wipe the toilet seat. Apply the brush to the toilet bowl. Wipe the mirror and faucet. Obtain and use a shower mister to coat the shower wall, curtain, and/or door.

Instill in your family the habit of making a bed immediately following a morning shower. The children won't be perfectionists, perhaps, but it's a start. A bed newly made becomes the inspiration to clean up other messes—clothes that need to be put in a hamper, toys that need to be gathered to a toy box, outerwear that needs to be hung in a closet, jewelry that needs to be returned to a jewelry box. The night tables tend to become cluttered. Now is the time to arrange them—and empty any waste receptacles, as well.

Family rooms, living rooms, hallways, entryways will probably be at the end of the list, but since they are the first things a visitor will see, they are no less important. Vacuum if necessary; dust whether it seems necessary. Bury magazines, pitch newspapers, or at the least straighten them. Put soft music on the CD and wipe tabletops and cabinets, particularly with evidence of fingerprints. If you have a coffee-table book, put it there. On a stand, fresh flowers are nice. Repeating advice from a previous chapter, ensure family pictures and mementos are packed away.

Thinking About Holding Your Open House

You now have your house cleaned and have taken steps to stage your home. You've done all the marketing you can think of and have placed a sign in your front yard. It would seem logical now to open your home to the buying public. If not you, who will? You are the agent now, and are totally responsible for all the steps.

Then you discover that few realtors in the area hold open houses. You know this because you are watching blogs from other interested home sellers.

It may be true. A disagreement exists whether a real estate agent is willing to conduct an open house. Some real estate agents show properties on appointment only. Look a little closer and you'll discover that every agent who does this is looking for the "big kill," that one high-end property that will provide a major boost to the annual salary. Chances are that you are FSBO because your property is something less than a multimillion-dollar estate.

Some real estate agents will conduct one open house, and no more, thinking because so many property searches today begin with a trip to the Internet, the better use of his or her weekend time will be to cull from the inquiries the handful most likely to wish to view *some* property, but perhaps not particularly yours. This agent has something in common with the agent highly interested in conducting open houses for you—references.

The agent who has a strong willingness to conduct an open house showing at your home—assuming he or she is the listing agent—will be happy to sell your home, but may be far more interested in gaining contact information from people who appear to view the home. An open house promotes a parade. Marching in this parade may be the one who would like to buy your home. Walking beside them are the few evaluating your home and several others like it in your area. However, the great preponderance of marchers are those who will gladly accept the agent's business card and anticipate a telephone discussion during the following week.

A good open house will attract many homebuyers, but not all will be qualified. Despite this ...

Open Houses Sell Homes

Let's establish first that having an open house is imperative for you. Remember, you are FSBO. This is something you must do for yourself. You don't really care that other realtors use an open house to expand their contact list. What you know is that you are not using a listing agent and because that, nobody is going to buy your home sight unseen.

Getting the potential buyer to view your home isn't the theme of this chapter. You can get many people to walk through your home. In many areas, spending Sunday afternoon "seeing how the other half lives" is a popular pastime. You're more interested in serious buyers and among those serious buyers you're more interested yet in qualifications to buy. Otherwise, your open house efforts become a social gathering where you are host to a band of curiosity seekers, or worse, somebody with more nefarious motives.

Preparing for Your First Open House

When you decide to hold an open house, don't make any serious Sunday afternoon plans. Sunday afternoon draws a more home-lookers. You want the maximum exposure, so you'd be wise to plan on at least a four-hour commitment, probably between the lunch and dinner hours. Your competition may be agents trading off two-hour shifts on Saturday and Sunday.

You'd like a day when the weather is pleasant, for many reasons. Buyers go to look during days that are warm and precipitation free. You don't really want people tracking water or mud into your home anyway. The downside is that you don't control the weather and your marketing commitments will have already been made; the funds have been expended. Schedule your open for a stormy day and you'll face cancelling it.

You might be smart to avoid holidays, community celebrations, and special events. You won't draw an audience on the day the local college basketball plays for a championship.

Sell Your Own Home

Twenty Safety Tips

The National Association of Realtors® offers a list of more than 50 safety tips for its members (Realtor® Safety Resource Kit). Not all apply to FSBO sellers, but those that do are offered here, reworded to apply to FSBO sellers:

Tip #1—Keep it light. Show properties before dark. If you must show after dark, turn on all lights and keep shades, curtains, and blinds drawn. Again, don't do it alone, but if you must, tell somebody you're doing it and ask that person to check in on you during the open house.

Tip #2—Checking in. Keep a log of visitors. Ask for name and contact information. Have your associate take note of license plates. Scam alert! Also, be alert to visitors' comings and goings, especially near the end of showing hours. Police have reported groups of criminals who target open houses, showing up en-masse near the end of the afternoon. While several "clients" distract the agent, others go through the house and steal anything they can quickly take.

Tip #3—Don't be too public. Advertise with pictures of the house, not with your picture. Don't divulge your full name (first, middle, last). Don't provide personal information that someone might use to access an account online.

Tip #4—Touch base. If you cannot find help for your open house, then establish a phone contact that will double-check on you. Call when the showing is complete. Set a lapsed time before the friend will call you.

Tip #5—Open house: it ain't over till it's over. Don't assume that everyone has left the premises at the end of an open house. Check the rooms and backyard before locking the doors. Be prepared to defend yourself, if necessary.

Tip #6—Stranger danger. Don't show your home alone. Not all buyers are who they say they are. Predators come in all shapes and sizes.

Tip #7—Sturdy doors are key to home safety. Make sure they have good sturdy locks.

Tip #8—Block identity theft. If your accounts have been exposed, place a fraud alert on your credit report. That automatically lets credit-card companies and other creditors know they must contact you before opening any new accounts or making any changes to your existing accounts.

Tip #9— Bring up the rear. One school of thought says don't stay with people walking through your home, as you don't want to pressure them as they envision themselves in your home. Others recommend that you should always have your prospect walk in front of you. Don't lead them; instead, direct them from a position slightly behind them. You can gesture for them to go before you and say, for example, "The master suite is in the back of the house." Either way, both sides are firm on this: don't talk much to the prospect.

Tip #10—Park behind. If you expect drivers to pull into your driveway, know that the exit for your automobile will be blocked. If it were necessary for you to run and jump into your car to get away, you'd be immobile.

Tip #11—Assure your cell phone service. Keep your cell phone where you can get to it. Test it within your house to assure yourself of service. If it were necessary to lock yourself into a closet, be certain that the phone will work there.

Tip #12—Fight or flight? Given the choice, run. Get yourself from danger and call for help. It's good business to have 911 on speed dial.

Tip #13—"Who's calling?" Most cell phones have caller-ID. If not, ensure you do have the service that will provide information about the source of the call. Avoid calls from "unknown" or "800 Service" numbers while you're doing your open house. Be cautious. People are not always who they say they are. Even using caller ID, you can never be too sure you know the caller. For example, if someone who claims to know you calls and starts to make unusual requests on your behalf, then *STOP TALKING!* When in doubt, test the call: if the caller has no recollection of previous conversations, then you probably should hang up.

Tip #14—Hide personal information. DON'T leave personal information like mail or bills out in the open where anyone can see it. Be sure to lock down your computer and lock up your laptop and any other expensive, easy-to-pocket electronics, like iPods, before your showing.

Tip #15—Agree on a distress code. Create a voice distress code, a secret word or phrase not commonly used but can be worked into any conversation for cases where you feel you are in danger. Use this if the person you are with can overhear the conversation.

Tip #16—Make a call. If you're feeling threatened, call. Besides 911, have several contact phone numbers where you can raise help. Stay calm; engage the person on the other end of the line with some meaningless dialogue, but might offer a clue that you're in trouble.

Tip #17—Have your excuse ready. Part of being prepared to deal with a threatening situation is having "an out." Prepare a scenario so you can leave—or you can encourage someone who makes you uncomfortable to leave. Examples: Your cell phone or pager went off and you have to call your office, you left some important information in your car, or you "just got a call and have to go pick up a friend."

Tip #18—Be careful with keys. Don't hand out house keys to friends, even if they are trustworthy. Know the location of all your house keys all the time. Never use hide-a-keys or leave the key under the doormat, above the door, in a flowerpot, or anywhere outside the house. You may think you're being clever, but experienced thieves know all the tricks. Also, keep your car keys and house keys on a different ring if you ever use valet parking or leave your keys with parking lot attendants or even at a repair garage.

Tip #19—Thwart thieves. Strangers will be walking through your home during showings or open houses. Remove or hide valuables in a safe place. Remove keys, credit cards, jewelry, crystal, furs, and other valuables from the home or lock them away during showings. Also, remove prescription drugs. Some seemingly honest people wouldn't mind getting their hands on a bottle of Viagra or antidepressants.

Tip #20—Rely on good neighbors. Inform a neighbor that you will be hosting an open house, and ask if he or she would keep an eye and ear open for anything unusual.

Setting Up the Trail to Your Home

Advertise, of course. As we've previously discussed, you'll have a greater draw from social media than from a newspaper. Put them in web ads and open house directories. Don't overlook the newspaper. Ideally, you should advertise the weekend before and the weekend of the open house. Check with the local paper to see when their ad closing deadlines are.

Set out your Open House Signs. If you're working with an agent that handles FSBO, you may be able to obtain some there. Otherwise, they are not difficult to obtain. If your house is on a thoroughfare, then signs a quarter mile away, in either direction should be sufficient. You need to put the signs at every turn, with arrows that point the way and gaily colored (helium-filled) balloons to draw attention. Be sure to check the sign regulations in your area.

These tasks must be accomplished before you can open your house for viewing:

Even if your home will not be listed with a real estate agency, if you desire to allow buyers' agents to show your home, then you should invite them to preview your home. Not only are you asking them to become familiar with your home, you will be able to get their inputs about your staging and pricing decisions. You should allow a week's lead-time, and this is the time for coffee and donuts in the kitchen. Convene a seminar in your own behalf.

Get rid of superfluous furniture. If you choose to hang onto furniture you value, simply because you don't want to move it twice, recognize that the visiting agents are looking for a home with as much space as possible. At the least, get rid of a third of what you have. You must make the home appear spacious. The rage for staging is becoming "prop" furniture, generally look-alike items that will not sustain weight. They come with wood-appearing finishes or slipcovers.

Anything that doesn't go with the house should be removed from the house before the open house. Out of sight, out of mind. If you feel the need to take your antique Westwood range with you when you move, remove it from your kitchen now and replace it will a suitable substitute. If the prospect doesn't see the item, it will not become a demanded contingency.

Part of preparing your home is removing evidence of pet occupation. Buyers are not interested in properties where there have been pets, partly because of residual odors. If you have decided to retain your parakeet, arrange for someone to care for the bird while the open house is conducted. A cute pet is a distraction from the point.

You need to prepare the literature—property summary sheets on the counter and by the entrance door, four-color fliers, or brochures promoting your sale. These will provide prospective buyers an overview of your home. You want potential buyers to carry away the images they have seen and the information that every buyer needs to know. How much was that home? How many bedrooms? How large is the lot? All these answers leave your home in your prospects' hands.

Property summary sheets should include information about utility costs and property taxes, and the history of each capital item—roof, furnace, air-conditioning, etc.

A couple of days before your open house, it's time for final cleaning. Clean appliance surfaces to a shine. Ensure your bedding is fresh. Vacuum rugs. Hang fresh washcloths and towels. Yes, make certain that the windows are clean, inside and out. Sweep out the garage and perhaps even the basement floor. Spruce up the outside. Trim the bushes; mow the lawn. Spic 'n Span is the word for the last tasks before showing your home to the world.

Sell Your Own Home

On the day before, you must now evaluate a basic question: the place looks so good now—do I really want to sell it? If you don't change your mind, then several things remain to prepare. Open the windows and air out the house, even in the colder weather. Obtain or prepare treats for your guests. Inspect your house as if it was the barracks for your troops (your kids), though you might not do the "white glove" examination. Prepare a log that folks will sign-in on when they arrive. You'll want to know their names and addresses, phone numbers and e-mail addresses. Of course, some will refuse to give that information, so if you can provide some incentive to obtain the information, do so. Prepare and display some feedback forms. Finally, prepare and distribute some fresh flowers throughout your home to add to the color and fragrance.

Prepare a Crib Sheet

What are the selling points of your home? Write them down. Do your best to memorize them. Use your seller's list as a crutch. Potential items include good school districts, recent renovations, property histories, "homesteader" benefits grandfathered to the property. New and major changes to the capital items in the house— the roof, the furnace, the water heater, new showers, new paint, and anything else that will impress. Make note of things that push the information "over the top," such as new windows, the R-value of insulation, and the acquisition of new appliances.

Emphasize the move-in condition of the house. Only "flippers," people who buy, renovate, then resell properties, are interested in "do-it-yourself" projects or "fixer-uppers." The rest are lazy, unskilled, or aloof. They don't want to do the extra work necessary to live in and enjoy the house. Think about the kind of "jack-of-all-trades" such a buyer might be faced with—landscaping, plumbing, appliance, and electrical work, they'll be reticent, even if the balance of the house is a dream, and the in-ground pool outside of the master bedroom is Olympic-size. They simply don't want to do the work. They feel when they drop six figures for a property, they ought to enjoy the living in that property for some time before they feel the pressure to upgrade.

Prepare a Teaser Sheet

Among the things you might want to make available to your open house visitors is a teaser sheet. A single page encapsulates the advertising that you didn't or couldn't do elsewhere. Here are points to consider:

"Walkable to ..." We're somewhat past the urban sprawl. People are beginning to move back to where it is no longer necessary to drive to get a loaf of bread or a gallon of milk. If your home is located where there is close-by, and by definition, "walkable to," access to shops or restaurants, tell your open house viewers. It may be important to know that a park with a playground is within walking distance.

Feel, floor plan, and flow. Advertising got your viewer to come to your home. It may have been on the Internet, in the newspaper, or the result of signs you have distributed. Or it is shown by a buyer's agent? However the prospect made it to you, consider describing your floor plan and room flow. Talk about movement among rooms. Talk about spaciousness of yard. Talk about the freedom to use a finished basement. This gives them a sales pitch to take with them, seeking their return with an offer.

Sell Your Own Home

First-timer upgrades. If your prospect has been living in an apartment or a rental, she could respond to pleasant visions, aspects of your home that would be attractive to her during the purchase of her first home. You can present information about upgrades in living style. You can talk about how quiet the neighborhood is. You can talk about the tremendous amount of storage space (we can never have too much). You can certain hype the aspects of lawn, backyard, deck, garden, BBQ, or other features of the outdoor life they might miss in an apartment. You might avoid discussion of snow removal.

Fancy finishes. If you have granite counter-tops, remind your viewer. Anything state-of-the-art bears mention—security system, surround sound, property lighting. Anything somewhat beyond the average home should be mentioned here.

Brand names. What mental image do you wish to leave with the viewer? Built-in California closets would draw such an image. How about Kenmore kitchen appliances? Or Sony sound system? Or Toshiba high definition with connections for Time/Warner cable service? Anderson windows? Jacuzzi hot tub?

Neighborhood names. Remind them of the upscale neighborhood where the home is located, particularly if the home is in a recognized and desirable area. Don't assume that all open house viewers will know.

"Built-in" or "custom." Remind the viewer of what items are built-in to your home, such as bookcases, custom furniture, storage systems, customized kitchen cabinetry, and little things such as a breakfast nook or a sunroom. Remind them of things they won't see elsewhere.

Environmentally conscious. If you are a part of the "green" revolution and your home reflect that—such as solar heating, dual-paned windows, xeriscape landscape gardening and watering, or rainwater harvester, remind the home viewer that your home is keeping up with environmental challenges. If you're into unique recycling, tell that to the viewer. It may be a new approach for the open house viewer, but one who may bring him back with an offer.

What's unique in your home? Special kitchen features, such as breakfast nooks, islands, and specialized and installed kitchen appliances? Is there a food preparation area or a secondary oven in the home? Does each bedroom have unique bathroom facilities? Is there something unique about shower or tub? Is there a hot tub or Whirlpool bath? A walk-in tub. His and her showers? Is there a mother-in-law apartment or room? Is the house on a corner lot? Does the living room have a cathedral ceiling? Is there a reason for a low heating or cooling cost? Whatever is unique about your home should be presented here.

What are you willing to discuss about the home's offer? Are there financing incentives? Are there closing cost credits? Would you be willing to move the house prior to repair for a lower cost? Will you pay the first year's homeowner association dues? Do you have a relationship with a bank should the viewer have no such connection? In this last category, whatever you can do to make the purchase easier will be welcomed by the viewer and potential buyer.

On The Day of the Big Show

Find elsewhere to park your vehicles; ask your neighbors to honor the parking space in front of your house. If not easily achieved, park your own vehicles further down the road. It is acceptable to keep one vehicle in the garage, but not in the driveway. That vehicle has another use, detailed below. Here are your open house day tasks:

Prepare a place for your viewers to "sign in." Gather names, phone numbers, e-mails, and any other useful contact information for follow-up. In keeping with concerns about security, it is recommended that a neighbor or a spouse make note of the car and tag numbers of your visitors.

Open all drapes, blinds, curtains, and any other window covering. You want daylight to stream into the home.

Ensure a good fragrance throughout the house. The lingering odor of recently baked cookies, which you will offer to your guests, might help. Consider you do not know of potential allergies of your guests, so you should avoid air fresheners or strong candles, which causes buyers to wonder what you are covering.

Illuminate the home—every light on. From this point, your home is a segmented sales room. Don't run exhaust or other fans. Silent, well lit, and clean are the bywords.

Put soft instrumental music on the CD player or stereo. Stores and restaurants use rock or pop music, or worse, for one purpose only—to encourage people to come in, shop or eat, and leave. Their money is made on the turnover. Think 101 Strings and light classical music. You want people to move leisurely through your home, picturing themselves and their children in the space you offer. Good music in each major section of the house can create a good mood.

Take a box and gather items of value—breakables, jewelry, money, heirlooms, account documents, checks, and other things that you must protect. Then, lock that box in the trunk of your car—the one still in the garage. Alternately, a bank lockbox might be useful. If, perchance, you're a gun owner, those weapons need to be secured and preferably hidden. You'd be wise to find a way to get them outside of the home.

Your four-color fliers with pictures of your home are on the counter. Consider creating a bulletin board that shows the outside of your home in each of the four major seasons.

If you can obtain financing literature from local banks, leave that information where the prospect can pick it up. It will help him or her determine a monthly mortgage payment.

Also, put out some or all of the following: Inspection reports, appraisals, user manuals, warranties for major appliances, descriptions of major repairs and the warranties involved, any house plans, blueprints, or literature regarding possible future improvements.

Serve refreshments or snacks. If you can bake some cookies, the house will smell nice. If you're well heeled, having a caterer might be useful.

Meet and greet prospects at the door. If the weather is good, leave the door open. If you must keep the door closed, post a "Please Enter" sign on the door where is can be seen.

Determine their interests. Make small talk about what they are seeking in a home and where possible, show them why your home will meet those needs.

Let people wander. Yes, they will open drawers and closets, and you will have to go around the house after they have left to ensure everything is again closed.

Be available when the viewers have questions. Give prompt, accurate, and complete answers. It should go without saying, honest answers. This becomes important because often, omitted or shaded answers become the basis for litigation.

Ask for feedback. Ask what they think of your home and whether they might consider buying it. No reason to be reticent. If they are willing to consider the home, you have the next step to take. If they are not interested, you'll not see them again unless they leave and return, having reconsidered their position. It's the only way you will get a direct answer and that might be the answer you want. From that point, everybody can sit at the kitchen table and draft an offer. Important point: get all offers in writing. Do not deal with spoken offers. Negotiation may ensue, and as we will discuss in the chapter devoted to that topic, when it's on paper, it's serious. Without commitments and obligations, it will never happen.

As part of your feedback efforts, a questionnaire or a return postcard could provide some insight about how to make your home more appealing to buyers.

Questioning the Visitors

You've spent time following a viewer around through your home. You've seen gestures and nonverbal language. You've overheard the observations. They may have asked questions.

Now the visit is over. The entourage makes its way to the front door to continue to the next open house. It's over. That's it? If you agree that the answer to the question is "yes," then you have lost some important feedback.

So at least ask, "What do you think of my humble abode?" Learning what your visitors think at the time they are leaving will be important to your future efforts to market the property.

"This FSBO is a new experience for me, and there's a lot I don't know. You can help me if you give me some insight into your thoughts as you have gone through my house." The risk is high when you ask such questions. You might learn something uncomfortable. You might learn some bad news. If true, that makes the questioning of the departing viewer important. Yet, there is a reluctance to do so.

Why? Do you think you've received dishonest feedback? You could. Are you afraid to hear the answers? Perhaps. You could find somebody reluctant to mention anything negative. Or the viewer might feel pressured to explain why he doesn't make an offer on the spot.

You need to hear what the potential buyer has to say. If you don't, you will continue to do something that could be changed, and you will never know why somebody rejected what you offered. You'll have no idea of what objection to overcome, much less how. You have a choice: you can try to do it in person or you can ask them to complete and return a questionnaire. The in-person interview is more effective, but at the least, don't let people leave without some literature about the home and a means to contact you. So here we go:

What is your impression? You want to hear the truth, but you'll probably hear, for the lack of a better way to put it, "faint praise." Don't agree to that on its face. If they feel negative, don't defend your house. Play sponge and soak up everything that can be said about it. Positive or negative, thank the viewers for their input.

How does this house stack up to others you've seen? Initially, you'll receive a comparison, but you can easily steer this response to learn exactly what the viewer seeks. Some of what they want, you might not be able to deliver. For example, she wants a house whose kitchen is flooded with morning sun, and your kitchen is on the west side. Learning how quickly the bedrooms will warm might be an apt response. If what you hear is a positive report, then exploit it: "Yes, that is my favorite room, as well. I love to sit and gaze out the garden window."

What do you like most about this home? Don't simply accept the positive points on their face value. Question the response. "What about the master bathroom do you like?" Or, "You seemed to like the kitchen cabinets. What are their best features?" One of two things will happen here. First, the person identifying the positive aspects of your home is actually explaining them to herself, and in the process may be convincing herself to look a second time and perhaps discuss the purchase of the home. Or, should that not happen, you now have a list of positive features that you can include in your literature or mention to any future visitor.

What do you like least about this home? Obviously, if the viewer didn't make an offer, something doesn't quite suit him or her. It may be room colors. It may be the wear of the carpet. It may be the nascent odor of a pet that you, accustomed to the smell, failed to clean. Get enough information from viewers and eventually common threads will emerge. Everybody knows that if necessary, *they* could paint the room in question, but they don't want to—they want *you* to know what color they like and already have it painted that way. Once you have several comments about the color of that wall, you may decide you wish to paint it before you show the home again.

What do you feel about the price? This may not be the first house the buyer has walked through. You know that you have established the price by comparison against other properties and by discussing it with a bank and perhaps an agent who works with FSBO sellers. You may have a home appraisal that tells you that it is accurately priced. However, to somebody, it's too much. Handle that person by finding what similar properties he's looked at and how he ranks the two together. Nobody will tell you the price is too low, but if the preponderance of the feedback is that people feel it is too high, you may consider repricing it. While you're at it, ask them what price they feel the house is worth.

How do you see yourself living in this home? Learn how they would rearrange the furniture. If they respond, you will have learned that they are considering how they would arrange the house to suit themselves. Once you know that, you can share with them what you've learned about room arrangements over the years you've lived in the home. If the prospect says that he or she can't picture occupying the house, ask why. If milady says she'd like a sewing room, you might be able to share how you could accommodate your crafting pursuits.

Would you like to make an offer today? It's a tough question to be confronted with on the spot, and that's the reason for it. The standard answer you'll get is: "I'll think about it." Follow with something like "What would it take for you to make an offer on this property? You obviously like it. We would like to sell it. How can we get together?" If they are amenable, you can cause them to discuss how they might make the property work for them and meet their needs. They are working on the problem; now you can focus on what you might do to help them meet your needs. A "hot prospect" might be willing if you sweeten the deal if they made an offer today.

Follow Up

If you have gone to the trouble to gain contact information, follow up. Yes, someone can easily dismiss you on the telephone. If you don't ask, you'll never know. You might catch someone who has left your home, looked at a few more, and is wondering where she put the contact information. Once you have determined an interest, you can take the next step, by inviting the couple to join you for "coffee and ...."

If you have evaluation sheets and matching contact information, you now can call and discuss the comments with the person. Always present it in terms such as, "We'd like to know what you think we could do to ...." You may well encounter the person who felt positively about everything but one item in your home.

However you achieve this, you may have one or more buyer(s) willing to sit to talk with you. You're now getting to the point about working with the buyer.

Chapter 4

Negotiating and Working With Buyers

If you want top dollar from the sale of your FSBO, be prepared to make an investment in your property before you put it up for sale. Home are lived in, and because of that, they deteriorate. We think because the tax bill increases, the value of the home increases, and that may not always be the case. The replacement value of the building increases, but it's actually the land on which it sits that increases in value.

What is this thing called Real Estate Negotiation?

How do we get the top dollar and best terms? The simplest explanation: "negotiation." Aside from the negative points of view of the phrase, it has come to mean "negotiation accompanied by shrewd bargaining and reciprocal concessions."

Negotiation sounds a bit scary, doesn't it? Draws up images of intense management/labor relations negotiations, where management promises a shutout should labor carry out strike threats. Those begin with some degree of hostility.

That's a bit different from the negotiations you're likely to encounter when dealing with one or more prospects for the FSBO you've begun. Those should not—though they sometimes do—involve any hostility.

When Negotiation Begins

Realistically, you've been negotiating since you took that first phone call following a newspaper ad, an Internet ad, or the FSBO sign on your front lawn. Someone expressed an interest in your property. There you stand with a smile on your face, the telephone in your hand, and thoughts running rapidly through your mind that somebody wants to see your house. However, selecting a mutually acceptable viewing time isn't the first negotiation. The first is that the caller has a list of available properties before him and is attempting to cull that list.

If you have done an appropriate job disseminating information about your property, then you have gone a long way to eliminate the nuisance calls. They know the location and features of the home and some information about the surrounding area. They may know the number of rooms, bedrooms, bathrooms, and what the heating and cooling systems are. They may have seen a visual tour of the home. They may have already driven by the home. They should already know the price of the home. You have already taken steps to invite only those with a reasonable shot at purchasing your home. Respond to the questions; volunteer nothing. Talk too much and jeopardize future contacts.

There you are on the phone with somebody who knows all this information and you have a singular purpose—get that person to make an appointment to come see the home. This is not the time to debate what the price is, what you're willing to do to help the buyer, how you can help the buyer find financing, what concessions you'd make to ease the buyer into your house, or to admit any deficiencies your home might have (we were planning to ...). Remember that the caller is seeking to eliminate your property from the list. That is at cross-purposes to your desires to invite the prospect to view the home. Therefore, the more complete your advertising is, the calls that prove useless can be discouraging. At least, you'll not waste your time.

Be responsive, be congenial, be patient, but *ask* for the appointment. Once the prospect has viewed your home, then you have a measure of his interest. Though you'll probably hear the *mother's response* ("we'll see") or another statement of delay, you should now have contact information, and should take steps to establish time for a second conversation. Who knows? The prospect may be willing to sit at the kitchen table and discuss an offer.

It's entirely possible that some telephone calls will be from realtor or real estate brokers. Some will be to entice you into *listing* your property. Deal with these courteously. Some will be from "buyer's agents." A buyer's agent is seeking to show your home to one or more of her clients. If you have decided that you're willing to deal with buyer's agents, you will wish to invite them to preview your home. They, in turn, will ask you to contract for their services, which boil down to a half-commission if they bring you the buyer. Ensure is not her right exclusively.

However you get to that point, eventually you hope somebody will be willing to make a bid on your property. It would be nice and simple if the prospect met your price and placed no condition on the transaction. If it ever happens, that will probably be the first time. No, now what begins is a dance of many facets: the price, home features, property considerations, financing considerations, inspection considerations, occupancy considerations, and no doubt many nuances among them.

Some Simple Rules

You've already proved that you have the tools to prepare, market, and show your property. Now, suddenly, you begin to worry about what is necessary to negotiate and close the deal. It's natural. You think you have to sell your house. You think some combination of words and deeds is necessary to persuade a buyer to offer on your house. If you were selling autos, cosmetics, or any kind of consumer products, you'd face learning all you can about your product then demonstrating the benefits to your prospect, asking a dozen different types of questions, and making merchandising decisions. The sale would depend on you.

Not so the sale of your house. Remember this: THE SALE DEPENDS ON YOUR HOUSE! *You* don't sell your home. Your *home* sells your home. The home will speak for you, and we have already talked about how your home can present the absolute best message for you.

Rule #1. The Goal is simply to obtain a signed purchase contract from this prospect. You need to keep the diversions from this purpose to a minimum.

Rule #2. Never, under any circumstance, accept an oral offer. Resolve at this point that everything you agree to be committed to writing. Remember that you and the prospect have divergent views. You want the highest possible price and the best terms for you. The buyer wants the lowest possible price with the best terms available.

Rule #3. Don't jump at the first offer. Understand that few prospects will meet your price, even if the price is inherently fair or altogether too low. There is something in the psyche that seems to dictate at least an attempt to obtain it for less. So among the early questions you will receive will be "Will you accept less?" or perhaps "Will you accept $xxx,xxx" (several thousand less than the advertised price). The rationale for this is simple. The assumption is that you have priced it high to provide space for reduction. Or it may be assumed that since you don't desire to pay a listing realtor's commission, you have room to "give."

Rule #4. This is a corollary to Rule #3: Always counteroffer. Repeat, *always* counteroffer. Do not simply reject the offer—that forecloses negotiation. Do not simply "split the difference." If you do that, you admit that you did set the price of the home too high. Listen to what is offered then specifically ask that they put the bid on paper for consideration. This is somewhat like the diplomat who asks for translation to his native language, despite his ability to speak the language, allow him time to think through his response.

Rule #5. Be armed with an accurate certified market analysis (CMA) that compares your home to comparable homes in the area, covering floor plan, number of rooms, square footage, upgrades, etc. Be armed also with a certified assessment—something other than what is done for property taxes. Once you have these two figures, you have the basis to counteroffer (sweetly, please) the lowball figure. As stated, if you merely tell them "no," the negotiation halts. You may lose the prospect, whose only objective is to obtain a property at a rock-bottom price, make some change in the property, and "flip" it to another sale. You probably are wise in your decision, but make at least one reasonable counteroffer to test the water.

Rule #6. Assist the prospect to take emotional ownership of your home. If you tell the prospect to prepare a written document, he will begin to perceive his family in the home. It's at this point he will begin to find a way to make it happen. It's a graduated ownership increase process. Questions such as, "What do you think you'd like to do with the kitchen?" will get milady on board. Similar questions to her spouse about hobbies will help the process. The fact that you didn't reject the lowball bid outright has started the prospects thinking about how they would fit with the property. They knew their lowball offer wouldn't fly, but they simply had to try. Because they are interested, they will continue to attempt to seek an acceptable middle ground.

These are the rules. There's more to negotiation, and we'll cover it. For now, remember this: no oral offers. No price-changing "back and forth" discussion. Ask the prospects to put their offer on paper. Offer writing materials and a cup of coffee and invite them to partake of both at the kitchen table.

Initially, the offer may take the form of "intent to purchase," defended by deposit or earnest money. After that, an official purchase agreement will be executed. Purchase agreements differ among political entity, state-by-state, and province by province. If you have obtained the services of a realtor who helps FSBO sellers, that seller can provide the forms. If you're dealing with a buyer's agent, that person should be a part of these kitchen discussions and the official documents that follow.

A prospective buyer may write different offers. If it's a buyer's market (many homes for sale in the area), there may be contingencies requested. The purpose of a contingency is to allow the agreement to be broken and any escrow funds to be returned:

It may be requested that the appraisal cover the sales price. If you already have the appraisal, it's now moot.

It may depend on the lender's willingness to fund the mortgage.

Allowances or credits for items to be replaced would constitute a contingency, but that must be worded according to the desires of the lending institution.

Often buyers in a buyer's market will request assistance to reduce closing costs.

Occasionally, the buyer will reserve the right to cancel if the outcome of a home inspection is unsatisfactory.

Buyers may request a home warranty protection plan that covers appliances and major systems in the home.

Buyers may also request a period to consider. Keep that period short. You desire to move the home. You need not be encumbered by an agreement on which the buyer may not act within a reasonable time.

Watch for the bargaining chip. Some buyers will ask for something to be left in the house. It doesn't matter whether the buyer wants or does not want your piano, your dining set, or another item. The buyer doesn't really care either. He wants something to release for a lower price. Don't get caught.

If it's a seller's market (few homes for sale in the area), the picture is somewhat different. Because of a paucity of inventory, many properties may draw offers from more than one buyer. Often a bidding war ensues and eventually the home may sell for more than the list price. An upper limit exists, however, and that will be the limit set by the lending institution.

Expect the prospect to submit a preapproval letter from a financial institution with the offer. A seller will be more disposed to deal with a preapproved buyer over one who does not have the preapproval but who offers a higher price.

The buyer in a seller's market may be represented by a buyer's agent, assuming you are open to such agency.

Sell Your Own Home

The rationale for this is that in a seller's market the buyer wants a "leg up" on the availability of property. Recognizing this and recognizing that the buyer's agent will be apprised of what is available within this buyer's specifications, the buyer will be seeking a positional advantage.

You can expect that a buyer in a seller's market will not make many demands. He won't insist that you buy the title insurance or that you vacate the house on the afternoon of closing. He may still incorporate some contingencies, but they will be for reasonable and explicable reasons.

In a seller's market, the buyer first with the most may be the one to score. You have no reason to consider low offers, so the seller won't play the game, anticipating a counteroffer. Often, the game becomes more important than the transaction. This buyer will have calculated the most he or she can afford and will offer that price.

Similarly, a large earnest money deposit demonstrates the buyer's seriousness. If you are impressed by this figure and all things being equal, if you feel the buyer has made a substantial effort, your risk will be diminished, as the prospect isn't about to simply walk away from a large deposit. The higher the deposit, the more serious is the buyer.

You may find that some buyers can pay cash for the home, even well into the six figures. They may have sold their prior home already, are living at the lake, and want to get into your home as quickly as possible. Alternately, the buyer can present so large a deposit on the home that he or she may be able to finance the balance exclusive of a mortgage contract. That has to be more attractive to you.

Depending on the legal jurisdiction in which you reside, the legal requirements may be for some inspections to be conducted in a specific period. Your willingness to ask the buyer to shorten those periods can result in an earlier closing on the property.

If the buyer is willing to shorten some inspections, he or she may waive some contingencies. They may be ill advised to do so. Despite this, some services are expensive and the buyer in a seller's market may be willing to indemnify those risks himself.

Expect the buyers to express an emotional attachment to the home. They may not send you a handwritten "love letter" about the property, but in many ways they will say they have "fallen in love" with your home and "can't wait" to get their furniture into the home.

Finally, because they are anxious to enter the property quickly, if you offer to close quickly, they may be amenable. This assumes that you, yourself, have a place to move to and have your own "ducks in a row." This will not work if you must attach your own contingencies to it. If you must also consider your own contingencies, write them into the contract. If you, yourself, are tied up in a contingency sale on a new property, you may face attempting to provide some incentives for your own buyer to perform.

Preapproval Letters

The serious house buyer will have taken steps to be certified by a financial institution as creditworthy to purchase a home. If he is in the market and has engaged a buyer's agent, his first step must be that letter of eligibility. Chances are that people merely walking through your open house haven't taken that step, so one of the tasks that may face the FSBO seller is the encouragement of the prospect to return with a loan preapproval letter prior to the commencement of negotiations.

Be careful here. You want to see a preapproval letter, not merely a statement that your prospect is prequalified. What is the difference? A prequalification is based on a lender's opinion—expressed because the buyer has a relationship with the organization—and it is not a certification that the lender has taken all the steps to ensure your prospect can buy your home. A preapproval letter has several benefits:

That prospect now will begin to look at homes he's serious about. He knows what the bank will provide and because of that he's not about to go significantly above that number and charge off in search of something that will prove to waste his time and yours. If he has engaged a buyer's agent, that agent is feeding him notices of properties that fit his criteria. If his criteria fit your home, he'll hear about it.

Because he is not "contained" in his selection, he is free to spend more time in homes that meet his parameters. He will look at your home more thoroughly than he might otherwise, finding those features he wishes to enjoy while identifying those where he'd like to change or improve.

Among a more narrow selection, he is certain to find one that "tickles his fancy." He's been told he's qualified to buy it and nobody is going to talk him from it if he really wants it. He may face stretching to meet the payments, but the place is his, once he has decided he wants it.

You the seller do not know what the buyer is eligible to buy. It is entirely possible that he may be authorized to meet your price but is willing to test your limits with a lower, yet reasonable offer that you may be led to accept. If he is successful, there may be enough left in the authorization to install that in-ground swimming pool he really wishes were in your backyard at this moment.

The closing is greased. The buyer has his authorization. The appraisal is done. You may have accepted his offer, and now all the bank has to do is to process the paperwork. Whereas it might have taken a month or more to do the closing in the linear manner, the fact that the buyer has his "ducks in a row," now moves your loan application to the top of the work file. You, the seller, faced with a buyer who can act now versus one who can't act for a month, might even be willing to shave a few dollars for the sheer privilege of having the transaction behind you.

All the prospect had to do to get there was to make the request, complete the loan application, complete the paperwork to allow verification of employment, list the assets, and collect credit data.

Now that FSBO prospect can prepare a purchase contract with the full assurance that of no impediments.

What Should Be In A Purchase Contract?

Several things should be a part of the agreement:

Residential Purchase Agreement form. Every legal entity has a form expressly for this purpose. Check with your real estate lawyer or with the buyer's agent to ensure you have the correct form. Your buyer has the responsibility to fill it out, but you should have the form in your hands. Ask what other forms must be completed now. Since you are neither lawyer nor real estate agent, not having the correct form(s) can lead to great difficulty.

Include the price. The buyer will need to specify explicitly a bona fide offer. No contingency offers are wise. Put the price in writing. Whether it's more or less than the asking price will depend on the direction of the market (buyer's or seller's). This number will be solely the buyer's responsibility.

Include the good-faith deposit/earnest money. The many ways to make this deposit include cash, personal check, certified check, personal or real estate, mortgages, or promissory notes. Anybody other than the seller may retain this deposit. Usually you will want your lawyer or a bank officer to hold it. Again, jurisdictions vary, but this deposit could be forfeited via legal "liquidated damages." You need to talk to a real estate lawyer.

The deposit is evidence against a down payment on the property. On this form, you must list the down payment and the form it takes—the options listed above. If that down payment will be the result of selling an asset, that stipulation may have to identify a contingency of the presentation of the down payment.

If there will be financing, the terms may be specified here, particularly if the papers are in order at the time the offer is made. The buyer may wish to specify a maximum interest rate, which if not achievable, becomes a reason and mechanism for nullifying the offer.

Contingencies must be specified here, including appraisals, inspections, mortgage funding. Except legal entities' requirements, such as requirements to remove lead-based paint, contingencies may be waived.

Spell out the possession requirements and any contingencies that apply. When will the buyer take over the property? On the day of closing? On the day following? If it will be prior to closing (not recommended), a rental agreement must be executed in favor of the seller. If it will be substantially after closing, and assuming all parties agree, a rental agreement must be executed in favor of the buyer. It is bad business to let a new buyer take possession prior to closing. Closings sometimes don't happen. New disqualifying discoveries are made. Financial arrangements fall through. Should you do it and something untoward happen, you're then faced with handling an eviction.

Fees, please—another reason to employ a real estate attorney at this point. Somebody will face paying fees for title, escrow, transfer taxes, etc. That somebody may be identified by local law. Otherwise, this agreement should specify either who will pay or how much they will be negotiated.

If inspections are an issue, reports requested must be a part of this document. Many jurisdictions have disclosure requirements, and those reports are mandatory. You, as seller, have a responsibility to make available all reports made on your property. Here again, your real estate attorney or your buyer's agent can advise what the customary requirements are in your locale.

Your buyer has been constructing an offer. There must be a limit to the time that offer remains "on the table." Again, varying by jurisdiction, there may be maximum and minimum periods, to accommodate sellers that may be from town for one reason or another. This section should clarify who receives the offer. Local contract law may have requirements about expiration.

Disclosures—the Good, the Bad, and the Ugly

If ever there were issues in the home that land the buyer and the seller in court, chances are high that disclosures lie at their heart. Not every jurisdiction requires disclosures, of course, but the number is climbing. Things that the seller must or should tell to the buyer that the buyer may rely upon are held on those disclosure forms. Agents are not allowed to complete disclosure forms, though some do, and when they do, they open themselves to some serious legal problems. You don't have an agent, so as the FSBO seller, it will fall on you to disclose several things, some required by national jurisdictions, and some which will be local — state or province.

Homes built before 1978 may contain lead-based paint, and the buyer has ten days to conduct—or arrange to conduct—an inspection for it. If it hasn't been removed and hasn't been waived, the potential exists for a lawsuit.

Matters of material fact must be disclosed, though the jurisdiction may dictate the period of coverage. Many require notification of deaths on the property. Deaths from natural causes are less a problem than violent deaths. In some places, deaths caused by AIDS must be declared. Your real estate lawyer is the one to consult.

Other items for disclosure is whether the home is on a floodplain, occasioned by tornadoes, near a geological fault, unique zoning areas, adjacent to fire hazards, or subject to excessive noise from some external source.

You don't have to identify accomplished major repairs, but why not? The buyer may be happy to learn that the sewer is new, that the roof has been replaced, or that the furnace or water heater is new.

How Much Earnest Money to Request

How much earnest money is enough? That can be answered in two words: "It depends." Earnest money is strictly a "put your money where your mouth is" action. It's a measure of the commitment a prospective buyer has to you, generally after he has seen the home, recognizes that others are interested in the home, and seeks a way to stand out in your evaluation of which buyer to select. It's particularly important in a seller's market, where the selection among multiple bids is up to you.

No specific law says what you can ask for earnest money. Varying jurisdictions may have differing advisories relative to the subject, but the only steadfast legal requirement is that the proposal to buy be defended with financial (or other) consideration. That consideration may be as little as a dollar or as much as an undefined percentage. It is customary for a seller to demand as much as 3% of the sales price as earnest money. In a buyer's market, the figure may be much less. The condition of the market and the custom of the local will have much to do with establishing the amount of the earnest money.

Earnest money is not a down payment. It may be the first *part* of a down payment, but technically the down payment is what a buyer must front in cash or other consideration to secure a mortgage for the balance. Theoretically, the *earnest money* plus the *balance of the down payment* plus the *mortgaged amount* should equal the agreed-to sale price of the home. That can be expressed as a formula: (SALE PRICE = EM + bDP + M).

Naturally, the prospect would like the earnest money to be as little as possible. It would be logical to ask why, since according to the formula he will pay the same either way. The difference is a little thing called *liquidated damages*. Most standard purchase agreements will contain a liquidated damages clause in case of default. The buyer can default in many ways. Perhaps he cannot obtain a mortgage. Perhaps he cannot obtain the balance of the necessary down payment to obtain the mortgage. Perhaps some untoward calamity has caused him to withdraw from the market for one reason or another. More likely, he has found another place that he prefers and is willing to forego the earnest money he has put on your house in favor of the new place more to his liking. Without the liquidated damages clause, you would be forced to refund his money. Woe to you if you've taken his earnest money and used it as earnest money for a new place.

Now the question becomes what the lending institution will do. If the lending institution is willing to accept the entire cost of the buyer's purchase of your home, it will be customary for the buyer to put down a substantial amount in earnest money, approximating the anticipated closing costs for the property. In a way, this guarantees that you, the seller, are protected against any slipups between the lender's agreement to fund the buyer and the closing process. Should the cost of closing eclipse the earnest money deposit and the buyer have no more, you now have to decide whether you, yourself, are willing to fund the difference.

Who Should Receive The Earnest Money?

Let's start this discussion with who should *not* receive the earnest money. That would be you. Do not accept any instrument payable to you directly.

Legally, anybody but you can take the payment, but that thinking often leads to misrepresentation and absconding with the money. Work with a real estate lawyer; he or she can receive the earnest money deposit. A buyer's agent can also be a legitimate recipient. Whatever reputable third party you select must place that earnest money in a separately maintained trust account. Moreover, it should be receipted. Once the contract has gone through and the transaction has closed, then you can request a release of that money.

Refunds on Cancellation

Are you obligated to return the earnest money? With no liquidated damages clause, you must. If the clause is in your contract, you need not. You have taken your home off the market. You have already paid the cost of marketing and staging, which costs would now have to be repeated for the second or subsequent cycle(s) of your effort to FSBO. If there is a liquidated damages clause and you choose not to require it, you can refund the earnest money. That choice is up to you. You may be sure the withdrawing prospect will make a great case for you to do so.

Depending on the jurisdiction, laws direct the steps to be taken. It is customary for the jurisdiction to specify a return period, should the buyer choose to cancel the contract. Again, this is extra to the liquidated damages clause. If you refuse to return the deposit without cause, there may be a civil penalty assessed.

Normally, when a cancellation occurs, you and the buyer will both be asked to sign mutual release instructions. If you cannot reach agreement, the money will remain in escrow, whereupon the holder of the money must communicate via a certified letter (USPS) or a registered letter (Canada Post) asking for instructions. With no response from you after the stated period, the money will be returned to the buyer. If you contest the action, the jurisdiction will hold that money for some period, after which it becomes the property of the jurisdiction.

Contingencies That May Affect Purchase Contracts

The magic words are "subject to ..." A contract involving the money required to purchase a home and the period throughout which there is a financial obligation subject to protections for all concerned. Of course, two of the parties are you and the buyer. However, there is a third party, and that is the jurisdiction. We'll get to the contingencies between you and the buyer shortly.

Contingencies involving the jurisdiction are largely code. Codes exist for foundations. Also, codes for electrical, heating, cooling, wells, sewer services, septic tanks, and leach fields. Disclosures are required for the protection of the buyer. Inspections exist to ascertain variations from the separate codes, but the jurisdiction may well dictate who is responsible for arranging and paying for those.

The Appraisal Contingency

Between the seller (you) and the buyer (your prospect) are several contingencies, most in favor of the buyer. Among those is the need for an appraisal. We've discussed before the wisdom of obtaining your own appraisal for a negotiating tool when you are contesting about the price with your prospective buyer. Lending institutions may require another appraisal relative to a mortgage on the property, and that, no doubt, will be the responsibility of the buyer.

A bank covers its bets. Mr. FSBO buyer may be financially sound and employed, well-enough heeled to purchase your $350,000 home. Somewhere down the line, the employer goes from business or moves to a more favorable business climate, the debtor cannot fulfill his mortgage requirement, and the bank doesn't want to find itself in the unenviable position of having committed so much money to a building actually worth a hundred thousand dollars less. The process is known as the building being "underwater." To ensure the home is worth at least what they are lending on it, institutions insist on a certified appraisal to cover its bets. That appraisal might be performed by an independent appraiser. The appraised worth of the property will determine the maximum a lender is willing to allow a buyer to mortgage, though that number may vary depending upon the size of the buyer's down payment.

The home appraisal protects the bank, but it also protects the buyer—it keeps the buyer from paying too much for an overpriced property simply because she was enamored of the beautiful view of the mountains from the picture window. A home appraisal is a numbers exercise, removing emotions from the calculation altogether.

A few things you should understand about real estate appraisals, for they are important to the sale of your home: It is through the appraisal that the property's market value is established. That may be the same thing as the sales price. You could sell it for more or less than the appraised value. If the property sells for less, then the buyer has made a gain. In some jurisdictions, that sale price may be used to reestablish the market value of the property, though you can be certain that the appraisal for taxes is entirely different. If the sale is made for a figure lower than the appraised value, the buyer has made a deal. Assuming the seller is satisfied with the deal, there's no loss to the seller. This is often the case where the heirs settle an estate for "whatever the market will bear." However, if the sales price is higher, expect the assessment for taxes and the market value figures will also increase. There is a caveat in that, also. Generally, the lending institution is willing to finance to the market value of the property alone, less any down payment. Its willingness to exceed that figure will depend on other factors, such as the projected growth of the area, the variations in local employment, or the extent of the credit-worthiness of the buyer.

The appraisal contingency is therefore straightforward. The buyer writes into the contract that the offer is subject to the relationship between the selling price and the appraisal or between the selling price and the willingness of the financial institution to establish a mortgage.

Appraisals/Comparative Market Analysis (CMA)

A comparative market analysis is different from an appraisal. The CMA is the tool normally used by real estate agents to help a home seller to arrive at a realistic asking price. An experienced agent might come close to the actual appraisal, but FSBO sellers are not frequently real estate agents at all, much less experienced agents. An appraisal will be accurate and is required by a lending institution to determine whether to lend money against a property.

An appraiser is a professionally trained individual and must serve an internship with more experienced appraisers. The lending institution may have an appraiser, but it more often will arrange with an independent appraiser. The purpose, of course, is objectivity. The buyer may often select the appraiser. The appraiser must have a history of accuracy that the lending institution is willing to accept. The buyer will generally pay for an appraiser when he has applied for the real estate loan, and, of course, assuming the purchase isn't for cash.

A logical question: Who pays for the appraisal? You, the FSBO seller? The FSBO buyer? The financial institution? Singular answer: yes. If you arranged for a pre-contract appraisal, a wise decision, that cost is exclusively yours. Otherwise, the appraisal is the lender's requirement but the buyer's responsibility. The payment, generally in the $300 range, is often included in the closing costs. Often as an incentive to act, the FSBO seller will agree to pay for the appraisal during the closing. Theoretically, that $300 is a drop-in-the-bucket relative to the total financial package.

The Contents of an Appraisal

In much the same way as a property is priced, the appraisal of your property will compare it to several similar properties on which appraisals have already been run. In the appraisal, expect to read about the local real estate market and how your property fits.

An appraisal is not an inspection, per se, but the appraiser will take note of items that will affect, negatively, the value of your property. There will be notes of deed and covenant restrictions, analyses of right-of-way conditions and access routes to the property. There will be comments about structural deficiencies, such as roof damage, evident mold, foundation problems, and often—where do-it-yourself (DIY) modification has been made—things that may violate area building codes.

The appraiser will also take note of the features of the home's location and any significant problems he may detect in the area. He will be in tune enough with the local market to estimate how long a property will be on the market. If you have arranged the appraisal yourself before a sales contract, that information will be valuable. If the appraisal is done to obtain a mortgage, that situation is already fait accompli.

How an Appraisal is Done

The first question might be who does an appraisal. There exists a Uniform Standard of Professional Appraisal Practice (USPAP) that details the qualifications for a professional appraiser and the techniques to be followed during the appraisal itself. The manual exceeds 400 pages and costs more than $100. You won't need to obtain one and you can be sure the jurisdictional requirements for certified assessments will rely on that standard. A lending institution may have an association with a certified appraiser. The USPAP is updated annually and its purpose is to ensure the opinions about your property are fair, objective, and consistent. Theoretically, under the standard identical houses should receive the same appraisal process, whether done in Toronto or Miami. It's important to note that it's the process that's consistent, not the result. Much of what occurs in an appraisal depends on local conditions and values.

While variations exist, expect the appraisal process will follow one of two primary courses. The *cost approach* is used largely for newly constructed property and focuses almost exclusively on replacement costs. Why replacement costs? What happens if the house is burned to the ground or flattened by a tornado? The bank confronts the same questions either way, and it may be a stipulation of the mortgage that the property be insured against such a loss.

The Cost Approach Appraisal

In a cost approach appraisal, the appraiser will note that the property address and legal description match the loan application, sales contract, and title documents and that the property address conforms to postal address format standards. It will identify that the owner of public record matches property seller on contracts, loan applications, and title documents. It will detail the occupancy status of the property as either owner, tenant, or vacant as of the effective date of the appraisal. It will indicate whether the property is offered for sale or was offered for sale within the twelve months prior to the effective date of the appraisal. It will detail the data source(s) used, offering price(s), date(s) and the days on market for the subject property. To the extent necessary, it will define the neighborhood as "Urban," "Suburban" or "Rural." It will describe the percent built up and the growth rate, including market conditions, housing trends, price and age ranges, and present land uses for the neighborhood properties. In the report, the appraiser will identify market trends and conditions, insight as to demand and supply, and an estimate of marketing time, if applicable. If flood zone data applies to this property, that information will be provided.

The Comparison Approach Appraisal

There is more to the cost approach, but this is probably less important to the FSBO seller/buyer than the second approach, the *comparison approach*. In this case, the value of the home is pitted against similar homes in nearby areas. It includes discussions of lot size, footprint size, square footage of the finished and unfinished space, the style and age of the house, the garage, fireplaces, and the backyard pool. Style and age are large determinants, because—as you will recall—the land appreciates while the building depreciates. The value of somewhat identical homes built fifty years apart may be significant.

Many of the same items are addressed in this approach. The home is where the mail service can reach it. From that point, things vary somewhat. Here are the things the appraiser will be interested to test in your FSBO:

The comparable homes recently sold or on the market are consistent with the neighborhood characteristics.

Size of the living areas and the prices are comparable to your property.

The public information for all reviewed properties is available for closed transactions between the contract and settlement dates of your property. The minimum number of comparable sales was closed before the effective date of the appraisal. The minimum number of comparable sales will be in your neighborhood, if possible.

Where possible, comparable sales must be recent. Older comparisons must be justified in the appraisal report.

Adjustments and improvements must be comparable, including site, view, age, and design. Some may be supported by market data.

The overall quality of the subject property and each comparable property selected are consistent with descriptions and photos.

Conditions of all compared properties must be similar. Variations must be explained by market data. Conditions must be given a rating that best describes the selected properties, consistent with descriptions and photos.

The appraiser may take pictures. They must be in color and match the description of the property. The photographs may be clear and reveal items disclosed in the appraisal report. Include pictures of kitchen, bathroom, main living areas, etc., taken from frontal positions and not from angles.

The appraiser will research the sale and transfer history of the subject property (three years back from the date of the appraisal) and comparable sales (one year from the last sale date). Consistency is the objective. Rapid increases in value due to renovations must be explained and photographed. Decreases in price must be supported by market data.

The Appraisal Report

The appraisal report generally includes:

- A description of methods used by the appraiser to determine the value of the property.
- The size, condition, improvements, materials used, and notes about the utilization of space.
- A statement of obvious problems—structural, moisture, pest infestation, appearance—compared to comparable properties.
- Site information—the neighborhood, the area, urban, suburban, or rural location, plot size and orientation.
- What the appraiser knows of the area's market trends that may affect the value.

- A comparative market analysis that supports the appraisal.
- Blueprints (if available), maps, photographs, and sketches that demonstrate the features of the report.

What (Ultimately) Does An Appraisal Tell You?

If the appraisal comes in "high," it means that your buyer has made a good deal and that the bank's concern has been accommodated. Theoretically, it tells you that you might have could obtain a higher price, but now that's a moot point. You desire to sell your home and the home is under contract. The appraisal, short of a natural disaster, means your sale will happen. What if it comes in "low?" A low appraisal can mean many things:

The lender will lend the appraised value and no more. Something to close the gap between what the banks will support and the price you wish to achieve, and which the buyer agrees to pay, subject to financing, is now necessary.

A low appraisal is prima facie evidence that the buyer is asked to pay too much for a property, at least in the eyes of the appraiser and the bank. It may not be such in your eyes, and emotionally you may have decided that you want your price and that's it. That works only if you are resolved to continue to live in the house. If you earnestly desire to sell the house, that means some things must change; the deal isn't necessarily over.

The first is obvious—drop the price of the house, particularly if the place is overpriced, and/or the bidding process has driven the home price up.

Next, the low value of the appraisal may be due to things that can be fixed, if repairs or maintenance can't be done. Once the changes have been made, you may be able to engage the appraiser to review them. There may be an additional charge for doing so, and, of course, that might have to be subject to the lending institution's approval. If not so and the buyer has no other options that can accommodate those changes, you may need to recognize that whether it's this buyer or another, those things will have to be changed if you are to maintain your price.

If you have doubts about the appraisal, you can order a second appraisal. This one will be at your expense. Sometimes an appraiser is unfamiliar with an area, but you should use one accepted by the lending institution. Should you choose not to do so, you can pursue the appraiser legally, but that would seem counterproductive.

If the bank won't fund the difference between the appraisal and the price and the buyer still wants the property, that buyer can make up the difference in cash. A low appraisal can still mean the lender will fund a mortgage, but it's only the first mortgage. A second mortgage or other financing instrument can still be a possibility.

Sometimes the price is bid up by the interest of several bidders. If the price was accurately established, there is little elasticity in the figure. The same reticence the bank has shown to this prospect will be shown to others. If the second, third, or fourth bidder faces the same question, there will be no chance to fulfill a contract with *anybody*, the contracts become void, the appraisal becomes dated, and you're faced either with dropping the price or remaining in the home. And the process begins again.

And Now Come(s) the Home Inspection(s)

Appraisers may report on the problems they observe, but their "inspection," if you'd call it that, is superficial at best. An appraisal is a different thing than a home inspection. An experienced home inspector indicates potential problems that mean trouble in the future. That inspector will test major appliances, examine the roof (also the attic area, if accessible), check the chimney, and verify the primary systems—heat, air, ventilation, electrical, plumbing. The whole idea of a home inspection is to ascertain that a home is in good condition before a transfer of title is achieved. It's a snapshot, a list of items that will need change, adjustment, or replacement before a sale can go through.

The problem with home inspections is the cursory requirement to be a home inspector. While home inspection organizations exist, the number of jurisdictions requiring certification or licensure is small. It makes sense that the buyer will wish to identify and utilize a qualified home inspector. Repeat that thought—it is the buyer's responsibility to arrange a home inspection, and, of course, pay for it.

Notwithstanding, you as the FSBO seller and he, as the FSBO buyer, may have little experience in using the services of a home inspector. It would therefore be good if you became involved in the selection of an inspector, because eventually you will be asked to change your home following the inspector's report. If worthwhile to mention, also, that you must insist on seeing the full report before responding to repair requests, for it is not incumbent on you to make all changes, simply because they are mentioned on the inspection report.

Of course, you must grant access to a home inspector. You must satisfy your concerns about that inspector having free and unfettered access. A few things you can do to assure your safety:

Look at an example of his work. Nowadays you can obtain a copy of an inspection report via an e-mail. Please request the inspector to redact any identifying information. Look at the size of the report. A comprehensive report will be between twenty and fifty pages in length. Be wary of a short report.

Ensure the inspector isn't merely a contractor in disguise, or recommends contractors. This is an area of possible conflict of interest, and there may be clues in the sample report.

Many jurisdictions request some form of certification or licensure, but no national standards exist. There is, however, an international organization, the International Association of Certified Home Inspectors Inc. (InterNACHI), a membership organization of home inspectors, with chapters in the United States, Canada, and elsewhere. They can be reached at E-mail: fastreply@nachi.org; Website: www.nachi.org

While there are organizations and courses of study for the inspection task, you still need references. Home inspectors should be listed with the Better Business Bureau. Ask for references and follow them up. Ask for certification and/or licensure documents, if available. If the inspector is a member of InterNACHI or another professional organization of home inspectors, you can check there.

A home inspector should be covered by errors and omissions insurance, and you can ask for evidence of that. Be sure to ascertain what is covered by that insurance, because the total of the liability may be merely the cost of the inspection, which, by the way, will lie between $150 and $500. Again, that cost is borne by the buyer,

A home inspector will find something wrong. It's inevitable. No "perfect house" exists, and even the new ones have problems. Ascertain potential charges for re-inspecting the home once the problems have been remediated.

You'd be wise to be there. You and your buyer should be there, not to chase the inspector around but (for you) to protect your assets and (for both of you) to receive an immediate oral report about items that really must be fixed. Once an inspection is done, the inspector can walk around the property with you to acquaint you with the mandatory and optional changes. Further, the inspector may suggest a pest inspection, something he is neither qualified nor licensed to do.

The Tasks of a Home Inspector

Expect a home inspector to check these things: the Foundation, the walls (interior and exterior), the roof, the attic (if extant), the basement (unless the home is on a slab or crawl space), the kitchen, the bathrooms, windows, insulation, and the major systems—electrical, plumbing, and the air and heating systems.

The inspection determines whether a property to be free of defects. This may reveal issues that may cause trouble with the new owners. He must know applicable local ordinances that apply to the property. In that regard, he is something of a building and code inspector, except that he has no enforcement authority. However, should he detect problems that are code violations, there are no limitations to what inspectors, buyers, and financial institutions can report to jurisdictional authority.

The inspectors tour the house, moving from room to room, examining the condition of the home. They may find large and small issues. The core structure will be examined, including the foundations, where they observe for weaknesses. Basements and crawl spaces are checked for possible molds, cracks, or seepage. The walls and flooring are examined.

After the structure is examined, the inspector will test individual utilities to ensure they are working. This will include plumbing, electrical, natural gas, and sewage services.

On the outside of the house, the inspector will check the roof, gutters, downspouts, flashing, and drainage. He will check porches, decks, garages, storage buildings, etc. for their integrity.

What Inspections of Home Conditions May Find

As the FSBO seller, you may face making repairs, based on what is found by the home inspector and any other inspections that may be done. It's important to recognize that these things are possibilities and if the deterioration is significant, your buyer prospect, once the sale is under contract, may reasonably expect that repairs be done, at least those that provide a danger.

The roof, floors, walls, windows, and structure may well need some adjustment; all are blessed with different life spans. Older homes are more susceptible, but the real issue is property safety. The seller always has the choice whether the repairs will be made. The buyer has the choice to withdraw from the contract if they are not made.

Sell Your Own Home

These are some areas where the inspection may likely identify areas where problems:

Wiring. Homes built through the 1950s were wired with two-wire ungrounded circuits. From 1960 on, three prong outlets became standard. For a while, homes were built with aluminum wiring, with many problems. Today, the requirement is again copper wiring and requirements on some circuits, notably those near water, for ground fault circuit interrupters (GFCI). While many appliances may continue to function on the older circuits, modern appliances and certainly sophisticated electronics require the newer circuitry. If yours is a home with the older wiring, your buyer might request that the home be rewired. If you are unwilling to do so, he may cancel his agreement.

Until about 1970, plumbers were still using galvanized steel pipes and lead solder. The result was that there was continue mineral buildup, rust, and leakage. It isn't necessary to re-plumb your home completely, but as these things occur, they will need to be replaced. An attempt was made to replace piping with polybutylene, but even those created problems and had to be replaced. Today you will see some cross-linked polyethylene piping (PEX), and that seems to work well.

Again, if the home is older, there may still be cast iron sewer pipes, though there will more likely be a fiber-based "black pipe." Known as the "Orangeburg" or "tar paper" (manufactured largely in Orangeburg, NY, Canada, and England, and widely used from the 1950s to the 1970s), this pipe began to break down and was replaced by polyvinylchloride (PVC) pipe and in some places by land tile. Today the PVC is widely used. Replacement of sewer evacuation piping is expensive, but may be necessary if a plumbing inspection highlights problems.

A sound roof is always a concern for a buyer, and the inspector may suggest a roof inspection. A roofing company will provide that service, if necessary. There may need to be adjustments, but replacements could easily be covered by a cash credit against a new roof when it becomes necessary. Be careful here. Hire only a qualified roof inspector. However, a roof certification is a strong selling point for the FSBO seller. That certification will discuss condition of roofing materials, the condition of ridges, caps, drip edges, drains, downspouts, gutters, and the flashing around pipes, chimneys, vents, valleys, and root-top heating and air-conditioning units. Included in the certification will be the roof, its age, its pitch, the number of layers (asbestos), and any obvious previous roof repairs. In many jurisdictions, this information is subject to disclosure.

Furnaces and water heaters may be at the end of their useful lives. A furnace is designed to last twenty years, a water heater for half that. Buyers have been known to insist on change of one or the other before they take possession of a house. The jurisdiction's code enforcement people will provide insight into this. Again, if they are working when the home is conveyed, there may need to be a cash credit against an eventual change. Similar concerns may be expressed about air-conditioning systems.

If the choice is to offer a cash credit or repair of an item—and that may have to be negotiated—you should remember that you are under no obligation to obtain the top-of-the-line replacements of anything or even the most qualified contractor to install them. A wise buyer might be willing to accept a cash credit against the home, pending the actual need to change the item, when he or she can obtain whatever equipment or contractor is wished.

Pest inspections are straightforward. The inspector is looking for damage caused by insects, bugs, termites, rodents, or dry rot. Many firms are licensed to do this, including national firms, such as Orkin or Abell. In this case, pest inspections cover only the accessible areas of the home and under the home crawl spaces.

Sewer line inspections are particularly important for older homes, and your FSBO buyer may be looking for assurance that the sewer is serviceable. If the home area is heavily populated by trees, sewer lines can be damaged by tree roots. A plumbing company can survey the line with a closed-circuit video camera, which they will install through a cleanout elbow in the line. You can watch it on the monitor.

Radon gas, the presence of asbestos (particularly around furnaces and heat vents), and mold are always concerns, and may be highlighted in a home inspection. Asbestos, of course, must be removed before the sale can go through. Apply mitigations for mold and radon.

Back to Negotiation

Up to now, we have devoted this chapter to the kind of things about which you will need to negotiate. The next negotiation process begins with your reaction to those reports, your buyer's pliability considering those reports, and the give-and-take whereby a new price is determined via a counteroffer. The first step is to decide exactly what your rock-bottom price is. Then take steps to better it.

There would be no "negotiation" if there were never a counteroffer. The reason should be obvious, but in case it is not, if the prospect makes an offer—which you know will be less than your asking price—that is not acceptable and you reject it out-of-hand, negotiations will cease.

Have the Facts Ready

It's easy to put your house on the market, so the tendency is not to do what might make your home sale easy. You need facts on your side—not only of the appraised value of your home, but also information about recent local home sales. Your CMA will provide that. Have the appraisal and the CMA available. Price your home above both, particularly in a strong market. In a weaker market, stick with the appraisal.

How would you go about presenting your home to a prospect? If you've done your research, you should have some idea of the kinds of questions to expect. "Rough out" the main points of what you wish to divulge about your home. Recognize that if you're dealing through a buyer's agent, you will be better prepared. You know your home; that agent does not.

Get a picture of the availability of financing in your area. Locate a current mortgage website and keep abreast of the daily terms. The more you understand what the buyer is against to obtaining financing, the better you can anticipate the rationale and the degree of the things the buyer would like to negotiate.

The buyer may be sincere—after all the homes he's viewed, he may really be interested in yours. Tell him no, however, and suddenly he mentally begins to review other, perhaps acceptable properties that he's examined. Your home is but one fish in a large sea, and unless you hold property in an extraordinary location or a constricted real estate market, he'll simply go on to the next. Indeed, the prospect may lowball his offer on the sheer supposition that you might accept it.

Reject his offer and the process begins again for you. The idea is to "not accept" the offer in favor of a counteroffer. You don't know, but that offer might not be as serious as it seems.

It takes a conversation. You put your home on the market for $295,000. You have an appraisal for $300,000, so you feel confident that any buyer should be happy to save $5,000. Your prospect, on the other hand, is confident that he can obtain it for less. So—review what you have told your prospect. Was there any way that you indicated you might take less? Did you tell him that you were taking a new job in a new city and have to pull up roots? Did you tell him that you have an option on another piece of property and therefore have a deadline? If you did, the buyer is confident to offer less.

Can you understand why the natural tendency is to go well below the appraisal? Does that mean that the buyer will be interested in paying $275,000 or nothing? That's probably not so. Time for a counteroffer. A counteroffer puts movement into the negotiation. Move a little and you send a signal that you're not set in stone. It is a strong indication that you're not desperate, but that perspective isn't yet sealed. It's an invitation for the buyer to make a more serious offer.

It would be fair to say that a home in which you've lived for some time has created a "pride of ownership" for you. You were the one who paneled the basement. You were the one who landscaped the yard. Whatever you have done to improve your property—professional or not—is something of which you may be proud. Because of that, it would be possible to take a low offer as an insult. Take the offer as a personal affront, and you undermine the negotiation. This is business, that's all. The best thing you can do is to be dispassionate about it.

You make a counteroffer and the buyer comes back with another offer, greater than the initial offer, of course, but still nowhere near what you would like to achieve. The idea now is to keep the discussion moving, both sides making adjustments. The investment in time and effort by the buyer brings him closer and closer to where a deal is done. Record all offers and counteroffers on the paperwork, by the way. That provides a transcript of your negotiations and becomes the method whereby you review all the steps every time either you or the buyer makes a counteroffer.

At this point, you must recognize that negotiation is a "game" and often the negotiators are caught up in the game, rather than what it represents. It's a fair assessment that the central issue is money—the buyer doesn't want to spend what you the FSBO seller are asking, though that figure may lie beneath the assessed value and therefore the loan value that the financial institution will support.

Usually, that money issue revolves around the 6% that you are now not going to pay a seller's agent because you decided to FSBO. There seems a curious bent for prospective buyers to offer the FSBO seller the price sought *less* than 6%. The seller is saving money; therefore, many feel that percentage should be passed on to the buyer. What they fail to recognize is that you chose to do the FSBO to save that 6% and if you merely give that to the buyer, you are no better off than if you had used a listing realtor and you were the one who did all the work.

You need to remain firm on that issue. Now, if you have decided to allow the participation of a buyer's agent, you have already decided to give 3% away. If you are willing to give that to a buyer who deals with you directly, now you have something that you can negotiate away—a half percent at a time, thank you. It's a part of the process of keeping it going, keeping the deal alive, working with the user toward an agreement. If you even suspect the FSBO buyer is working through a buyer's agent, insist that the discount apply to that agent alone.

Anticipating The Buyer's Gambits

Once you have a purchase agreement, expect several actions by the buyer. Take a breath, think it through, and speak slowly and deliberately.

It's commonly called "the higher authority." The buyer wants to use someone else to "review" the contract before going through with the deal. It may be his parents; it may be his lawyer; it may be anyone outside the closed circle of the negotiators. The purpose is to create some discomfort that would cause you to reduce the price. Respond to this with a question: "Is there anyone else who should be a part of this negotiation?" Your buyer isn't going to delay the negotiation and he has learned that you are willing to do so. If he answers affirmatively, have the party called. If he says no, proceed but repeat that the negotiation will be between you. If there will be another party to the negotiation, and if you are willing that he is present, discontinue all negotiations until all parties are present. Understand that anybody other than the buyer who becomes a part of the negotiation becomes an advisor to the buyer—an alter ego.

Some buyers are "nibblers." A nibbler will try to reduce your price over little things, and one thing is never enough. Once that agreement is signed and you have a price, the nibbler will want to modify the obligations. Document everything—every desire, every response—and each time, review the process. If the buyer still wants a change, you must decide whether it is a deal-breaker—you can always walk away. Below you will see emotional reactions.

Often, the buyer will interrupt the negotiations with an off-the-wall offer: "Will You Accept (a figure)." Of course, whatever the figure is will favors the buyer. You need time to think. Do not react. Ask for the offer to be given in writing. It takes away the necessity for an immediate decision and provides time to think it through.

Do not allow yourself to become the respondent to a barrage of buyer's questions, asked to build a hedge around you. Be polite, but recognize that none of his questions will lead to a commitment. He's attempting to get you to commit to an idea or a figure without being totally aware. Respond with a question that replaces the onus on the buyer. That question will take the form of: "If I did, would you (do)?"

What Can You Do?

Begin with a fair price—the appraisal or less. The price can increase with multiple bidders, but this is not strictly a financial transaction for you. If you start with a fair price, you will elicit fair counteroffers.

The buyer has concerns and issues of which you may not be aware. Gradually, those issues will become evident. The FSBO seller who understands and respects what is important to the buyer can achieve more success.

Sell Your Own Home

Ask yourself "What's important?" Not every issue is major. Concessions on minor issues build understanding and support. If they become sticking points, set them aside. Document them so both of you are assured they are covered, but when the process is drawing to a close, revisit them; you'll find they are much less important.

The whole concept of negotiation is compromise. That's not necessarily the split down the middle, but the entire concept of give-and-take. Hopefully, when the process is complete, the buyer and seller will both be convinced that it was a "fair deal."

Other ways you can work with your buyer to make the deal more palatable: Your home could use a coat of paint and you haven't had time to see that done—or it's not a good season for doing so. You recognize that it's one of the things a FSBO seller should do, but it didn't work out the way you had hoped. It can now be a concession—a few hundred dollars against a moderate six-figure sale. That can be a counteroffer.

Perhaps your buyer needs to move in quickly for his children to begin the new school year. It's the latter part of August and you won't be able to leave the area, if that's your plan, until the second week of September. Would it be a good tradeoff to keep the price where you last placed it but be willing to put a few things in temporary storage and take a temporary residence until your affairs are cleared here? That can be a counteroffer.

Here is a caution—because negotiation may be an uncomfortable activity, it's a natural tendency simply to split the difference. There's plenty of advice out there that recommends against that, for no reason other than you will receive too little for your property. It's further testimony to your buyer that you set the price too high. If you feel the need to go lower for some reason, offer something in lieu of a price reduction—assistance on the closing, for example. Or prepaid insurance. Or a piece of furniture that the buyer admired and you don't mind leaving. Concede, but make your concessions minor with each repetition. Remember, the idea is to keep the discussion going.

Here's a beneficial technique: always be the one to "give up" reluctantly, and try to give up non-price value first. When you concede some little thing, the buyer will feel he has won because he made the suggestion or the request. If the buyer is the one who has requested to split the difference, don't simply do it—but don't give up on the idea, because you may be able to split the difference a second time, and that figure may be close to your bottom line. The concept is clear, if the house is listed for $100,000 and the buyer offers $50,000, counteroffer at $75,000 if that number is above your bottom line. If it isn't, keep your reductions minor and progressive.

Because negotiation can be a game, the assumption is that it could become a "power game." You, as FSBO seller, must be willing to walk away. It's your property. You maintain the power. You may wish to negotiate, but when the point comes that you can go no further, do not hesitate to cut off discussion and close the offer. By that time, the buyer has a lot invested emotionally. His family has now begun to see itself in your home. If you back away from a concession or withdraw an offer to do something besides what you have previously offered, it's a gamble but one where you evidence strength. Can the buyer withdraw? Yes, of course. Whether he does at this point will depend how emotionally involved he is with your home.

Then, keep something dramatic available that you're willing to give or do as a clincher. One suggestion might be that you'll be willing to pay the current tax bill. The money is in escrow anyway, so it's not like you're taking it from your wallet in the heat of the negotiation process.

Chapter 5

Reaching Agreement and Closing Your Sale

Do You Need A Lawyer?

Yes. The FSBO must not be his own lawyer. In some jurisdictions, having a lawyer available is mandatory. The sale of a home is fraught with traps for anyone with little or no experience. If nothing else, a qualified real estate lawyer will protect from an unscrupulous buyer. Legal issues and problems do arise. You want the largest proceeds from the sale of your home, but you must balance the lawyer's fees with the probability of loss if something goes awry. The lawyer will ensure that your rights and financial interests are protected.

It is important to select a lawyer who knows about and is experienced in real estate law. It is not to your advantage to hire an inexpensive lawyer who has only recently hung a shingle.

If you had taken on a listing agent, getting a lawyer involved early would have been wise. As for a FSBO seller, you have a little time, but you might be wise to involve him from the point of the first offer. He'll be with you through almost all the steps if you do. If it's done with sufficient lead-time, you may be able to engage the attorney of your choice.

Why so early? Contingencies and stipulations, conditions of sale; many and variations of techniques that permit a prospect to cancel the sale with impunity. Many who might be interested in your home may be professional "flippers." You may be assured that they have precisely the wording they want included in their purchase agreements. They buy and sell homes for a business and are adept at engineering terms most favorable to themselves. You need a lawyer on your side to protect your interests. Further, having your own lawyer will keep issues of detail straight and without error. If something occurs that engenders a dispute, he is your champion.

One of the areas of benefit to the FSBO seller available from an experienced real estate lawyer will be the inclusion in your agreements for conditions that must be met or escape clauses you may need. The buyer isn't the only one to want those. If you aren't in a hurry, agreeing to a potential buyer's conditions could tie you up indefinitely. Your lawyer can help write the contract so that you don't have to wait an extended time for the conditions to be met. This will allow you to avoid rejecting an offer, but may be worded such that you can accept and consider meanwhile. Worded correctly, should you receive a better offer, you would have the right to ask the buyer to cancel his condition and consummate the original contract. Alternatively, this can also contain a right of first refusal.

Another reason to involve a lawyer would be the "relocation condition." This would allow you to escape your contract if in your new location you cannot consummate a purchase agreement on a property of your choosing, and therefore have nowhere to move.

The Closing

Closing, often called a settlement, is the final step in the real estate transaction process. At this stage, you really need available a real estate lawyer, as the forms to be completed and filed with a variety of jurisdictions are lengthy, complicated, and extensive. This is not the place to try to do it yourself, no matter what you may find on the Internet or in a DIY forms package from the stationery store. Do this step wrong and you'll be in significant trouble. Fortunately, many jurisdictions require using a lawyer.

Where you do your closing is significant, as well. Rules can change from state to state, province to province. That commonly done in one part of the country may not be done countrywide. In this chapter, we'll hit the highlights as they apply to the FSBO situation, but recognize that this is not the complete manual of what you should do to close the sale of your property.

Recall that since that first offer, you and your buyer have been negotiating the final purchase contract. All the negotiation you have done has taken you from that first written offer to a completed purchase contract. It's time now to take the steps to transfer the ownership of the property to the buyer. Under normal circumstances, the process occurs when a seller transfers a deed to the buyer. Were that it was as simple as that.

No, what now occurs is a series of steps largely in the purview of the financial institution involved, unless this has been strictly a cash sale. Lenders who provide financing to the buyer as a mortgage will often require that a title company become involved. The title company will conduct a title search, arrange title insurance for the buyer's protection, arrange an appraisal if that has not already been done, and coordinate with one or more real estate attorneys representing both the seller and the buyer.

During closing, these things will occur:

- The buyer and/or his lender will prepare and deliver an instrument of value for the balance owed on the purchase price of the home. Normally, this will be a certified check, but it could be done via an electronic transfer, depending on the distances involved. It's important to recognize that this is the balance for the home itself, and has no resemblance to the total amount of the loan. In the case where the loan proceeds plus the earnest money previously paid do not fulfill the purchase price, the buyer's certified check for the difference will be prepared, as well.

- Assisted by the real estate attorney, the seller will endorse the deed to the buyer (or financial institution). The seller's signature must be notarized and the deed will be recorded in the legal jurisdiction. A mortgage will also be recorded then.

- Possession by the buyer occurs when the seller hands over the keys to the home. Under normal circumstances, delivery of the keys is done at closing time, but that presupposes that the seller has moved out and the home is available for possession. If it's a matter of a day or two, that situation may be handled by agreement. If the time is longer, the date of possession would have to be stipulated in the purchase agreement contract.

- Again, where you are dictates the protocol, but at this point a real estate attorney or a title company will normally arrange registration of the new deed with the legal jurisdiction. Accumulated real estate taxes will be prepaid, some insurances will be required, and recorder's fees, part of the closing costs, will have to be settled by that time. Further, any other changes for escrow, title companies, and buyer's agent fees will be settled then.

- Throughout this book, we have assumed that the FSBO seller owns his property outright. The truth of the matter is that you may still have an outstanding mortgage on your property that must be settled as this transfer is made. If so, what you, the seller, would now receive would be a bank transfer of the proceeds of the sale, minus closing costs and the payoff on your own mortgage.

At This Point, a Review

When the real estate transaction is negotiated, the terms established form a property contract that identify both the seller and the buyer, a description of the property, the closing date, and the price. You took the offer, turned it into a pre-sales contract, modified the contents with each offer/counteroffer, and eventually that document became the agreement between you. If there are contingencies, their possibilities must be detailed in the agreement, and once executed, that contract becomes legally binding on both parties.

Any changes to that contract must be by agreement, unless automatically broken by the death of one of the parties, and it becomes a function of the deceased party's estate, not applicable to our discussions here. It would be fair to say that the potential buyer has more opportunities to break the contract than the seller. The inability to obtain financing is a very strong contingency for breaking the contract, for example. Another would be the failure of the seller to respond to an inspection within a contracted period. However, it is impossible unilaterally to modify the agreement. However, a counteroffer is considered a new offer, invalidating the previous contracts.

In either case, the binding contract has consideration—a deposit of cash or other negotiable instruments. Once the contract has been created, the ownership of that deposit depends on both parties operating within the agreement.

The last signatory to the contract makes it official, and it becomes binding when delivered to the other party. As the FSBO seller, you should be prepared for the buyer to build withdrawal contingencies into the contract. Remember, that the whole reason for doing so is to ensure that deposits tendered against the property are returned to the buyer if there is a discontinuance of the agreement.

The alternative is civil litigation, which might make the attorneys happy, but won't do much for you. That civil litigation may cause the deposit to be awarded to the injured party. That's a function of contract law, and you would need legal advice.

Renegotiation is an option. Normally, that involves a reduction in price, and is generally caused by a property appraisal below the sale value on the property. Alternatively, the property inspections may raise issues which the seller in unable to respond to, such as those requiring the expenditure of significant sums of cash. Then, the two parties may agree on a lower price, after which the buyer accepts the responsibility to fix the problems.

There are certain other conditions where the contract is unenforceable. These include the incapacity to make a legal contract, or where it can be proved that one party is mentally impaired or incompetent. If no consideration has been provided, the contract is not enforceable. Fraud is involved. If the title to the property is not in the name of the contracting party, the contract is void.

Disclosure

Just as the bank does not wish to back a worthless asset, neither does the buyer of property. The buyer does not wish to purchase a home just to find there are major deficiencies, some of which might even border on fraud. To foreclose such a possibility, jurisdictions of state or province have instituted disclosure statements. The rules vary by jurisdiction, however, and often begin like this:

"Seller states that the information contained in this Disclosure is correct to the best of Seller's CURRENT ACTUAL KNOWLEDGE from the date indicated. The prospective buyer and the owner may wish to obtain professional advice or inspections of the property and arrange for appropriate provisions in a contract between them concerning any advice, inspections, defects, or warranties obtained on the property. The representations in this form are the representations of the owner and are not the representations of the agent, if any. This information is for disclosure only and is not intended to be a part of any contract between the buyer and the owner. An owner must complete and sign the disclosure form and submit the form to a prospective buyer before an offer is accepted for the sale of the real estate."

Note two things: first, the owner must complete the form—the agent is not permitted to do so. Second, the buyer must agree to the disclosures before an offer can be accepted. Thus, if inspections determine problems that must be addressed, and if both owner and buyer agree, they will be passed on to the buyer, those deficiencies must be disclosed and accepted by the buyer.

Sell Your Own Home

By whatever form you use, there will be several sections that deal with the various parts of the property. In this first example, questions are asked about appliances in the home—what ones exist, are they defective, or if it's not known. By "defective," it is meant that a condition exists that would seriously impair the health and safety of future occupants of the property, or if not repaired, removed, or replaced would significantly shorten or adversely affect the expected normal life of the premises.

A. APPLIANCES	None/Not Included	Defective	Not Defective	Do Not Know
Built-in Vacuum System				
Clothes Dryer				
Clothes Washer				
Dishwasher				
Disposal				
Freezer				
Gas Grill				
Hood				
Microwave Oven				
Oven				
Range				
Refrigerator				
Room Air Conditioner(s)				
Trash Compactor				
TV Antenna / Dish				
Other:				

It's important to note that just because an appliance is listed, this does not infer that all those will remain with the home. The owner is not going to remove a built-in vacuum system, for example. Chances are that the dishwasher and disposal will also remain. Most buyers expect the range and refrigerator to stay with the house. The other items are available for negotiation, assuming the buyer knows they exist. Remove from the home those items that will not be a part of the sale.

Next are the major electrical systems. Not all will apply to your home, of course. Alarms and detectors are generally considered appurtenances to the home and stay. If you don't want the garage door opener to stay, remove it before your home goes on the market. Often you can substitute things—fancy switch plates, for example—but you should do so before you put your home on the market.

B. ELECTRICAL SYSTEM	None/Not Included	Defective	Not Defective	Do Not Know
Air Purifier				
Burglar Alarm				
Ceiling Fan(s)				
Garage Door Opener / Controls				
Inside Telephone Wiring and Blocks / Jacks				
Intercom				
Light Fixtures				
Sauna				
Smoke / Fire Alarm(s)				
Switches and Outlets				
Vent Fan(s)				
60 / 100 / 200 Amp Service (Circle one)				

Next on the disclosure are the water utilities. For many locations, water-conditioning appliances are considered a part of the home. Some caution is useful here, as well. An older home in a more modern suburb could easily have a septic system, despite the availability of municipal sewer services. If that is the case, then the owner may have avoided connection fees. As the FSBO seller, you must be unscrupulously honest about these issues, else they can come back to bite you legally.

C. WATER & SEWER SYSTEM	None/Not Included	Defective	Not Defective	Do Not Know
Cistern				
Septic Field / Bed				
Hot Tub				
Plumbing				
Aerator System				
Sump Pump				
Irrigation Systems				
Water Heater / Electric				
Water Heater / Gas				
Water Heater / Solar				
Water Purifier				
Water Softener				
Well				
Septic & Holding Tank/Septic Mound				
Geothermal and Heat Pump				
Other Sewer System (*Explain*)				

	Yes	No	Do Not Know
Are the improvements connected to a public water system?			
Are the improvements connected to a public sewer system?			
Are there any additions that may require improvements to the sewage disposal system?			
If yes, have the improvements been completed on the sewage disposal system?			
Are the improvements connected to a private/community water system?			
Are the improvements connected to a private/community sewer system?			

Next, within the home itself, the items that apply to the comfort systems—heating, air-conditioning, and water heating. Again, you may not need to leave a stand-alone dehumidifier, but the gesture is welcome and the cost is insignificant. Humidifiers may be a feature of the furnace system. Don't plan to remove solar panels from the roof or generator connections from the garage. The generator itself may travel with you, but could become a negotiating chip for your discussions with your buyer.

D. HEATING & COOLING SYSTEM	None/Not Included	Defective	Not Defective	Do Not Know
Attic Fan				
Central Air Conditioning				
Hot Water Heat				
Furnace Heat / Gas				
Furnace Heat / Electric				
Solar House-Heating				
Woodburning Stove				
Fireplace				
Fireplace Insert				
Air Cleaner				
Humidifier				
Propane Tank				
Other Heating Source				

Roofs and hazardous conditions are next. The form doesn't identify the type of roof, and that may or may not be relevant to the purchase. For the state that posed this form, however, it assumes that most roofs are asphalt shingle or tar paper. Slate, shake, and tile roofs might not conform to this form, however, yet evidence damage. This is one of the reasons for having a certified roof inspector examine the roof of your home. Note that jurisdictions may have restrictions on the age of the roof or on the courses laid-on, for asphalt shingles.

2. ROOF	YES	NO	DO NOT KNOW
Age, if known: _____ Years.			
Does the roof leak?			
Is there present damage to the roof?			
Is there more than one roof on the house? If so, how many layers? _____			

3. HAZARDOUS CONDITIONS	YES	NO	DO NOT KNOW
Have there been or are there any hazardous conditions on the property, such as methane gas, lead paint, radon gas in house or well, radioactive material, landfill, mineshaft, expansive soil, toxic materials, mold, other biological contaminants, asbestos insulation, or PCB's? Explain:			

E. ADDITIONAL COMMENTS AND/OR EXPLANATIONS: (*Use additional pages, if necessary*)

The list given for hazardous conditions is self-explanatory. Note that it concentrates on conditions on the property itself, and take no note of similar conditions in the proximity.

What other disclosures apply? Note that the first given applies to aluminum wiring, previously mentioned. The balance of the form addresses various problems that might crop up—access, problems with prior improvements, structural changes, etc. Your jurisdiction may be more stringent compared with these items:

4. OTHER DISCLOSURES	YES	NO	DO NOT KNOW
Do improvements have aluminum wiring?			
Are there any foundation problems with the improvements?			
Are there any encroachments?			
Are there any violations of zoning, building codes, or restrictive covenants?			
Is the present use a non-conforming use? Explain:			
Is the access to your property via a private road?			
Is the access to your property via a public road?			
Is the access to your property via an easement?			
Have you received any notices by any governmental or quasi-governmental agencies affecting this property?			
Are there any structural problems with the building?			
Have any substantial additions or alterations been made without a required building permit?			
Are there moisture and/or water problems in the basement, crawl space area, or any other area?			

Have any improvements been treated for wood destroying insects?			
Are the furnace/woodstove/chimney/flue all in working order?			
Is the property in a flood plain?			
Do you currently pay flood insurance?			
Does the property contain underground storage tank(s)?			
Is the homeowner a licensed real estate salesperson or broker?			
Is there any threatened or existing litigation regarding the property?			
Is the property subject to convenants, conditions and/or restrictions of a homeowner's association?			
Is the property located within one (1) mile of an airport?			

Certainly, by now the buyer knows if your home is within a mile of the airport, so why ask the question. Aside from the crash potential—for which there will be differences in insurance rates—there may be deed restrictions about the erection of towers on the property, something that might be of tremendous importance to a radio amateur.

Note the existing litigation question—one of the reasons the buyer is careful and the financial institution demands a title search is the potential for liens on the property. Workmen's (or Mechanic's) liens will insist on payment from the proceeds of the sales transaction.

Finally, the disclosure will identify that it has been furnished by the seller, who certifies to its true based on his CURRENT ACTUAL KNOWLEDGE. It will identify that the disclosure form is not a warranty by the owner and the disclosure form may not be used as a substitute for inspections or warranties that either the buyer or the seller may later obtain. At or before the settlement, the owner must disclose any material change in the condition of the property or certify to the purchaser at settlement that the condition of the property is substantially the same as when the disclosure form was provided. Both Seller and Buyer will sign and date the form.

The Forms, the Forms

That's the form from one jurisdiction, but hardly the extent of disclosures you should make. Do not, under any circumstances, assume that just because you've satisfied the jurisdictional disclosure mandates, that's all there is. There are other disclosures to make; if you don't, you're gambling that the sale is firm or that. Anything less than a full disclosure exposes you to costly risks.

Unfortunately, with a good cause, it pays to either fix it or declare it; in some cases, you'll pay to fix it anyway. An example might be a paneled basement where the paneling covers cracks in the foundation. There have been instances where it has happened, and the seller has kept his fingers crossed that the issue would not be discovered.

However, deficiencies in the house itself may not be the only disclosure. Some jurisdictions recommend that noisome neighbors or pets should be disclosed.

A few things will be beneficial for the FSBO seller to disclose:

Repairs made to your property should be disclosed. Does the sewer line need a periodic visit to remove tree roots? Is there a depletion of the aquifer under the property that required the home to be shored up? What cracks have appeared in the foundation and how have you responded to them?

Sell Your Own Home

Repairs to major services—roof, plumbing, electrical, heating, and cooling systems need services, yes, but the need to expand the amperage of the electrical supply should be declared. If you know that the last time you turned on the air-conditioning it didn't work, you need to tell the prospect.

Deficiencies exposed by prior owners—have they been dealt with or are they still extant?

Pests are a problem. If the property has a history of termite and treatments, that should be disclosed. It's one thing to take over a property and know some form of regular maintenance is necessary. It's quite another to discover an infestation that looks like it's not new. Of course, it is smart to obtain a termite inspection, and your buyer just might add it to his list.

Water damage and mold. Did the roof leak? Was there water damage, and can it still be observed? What did you do to fix it? If there is dampness and you've taken steps to control it, you would have no worry. However if you took out the dehumidifiers during the open house and the buyer discovers that seepage and mold form in the basement or in the exterior walls, you may be asking for trouble if it hasn't been disclosed.

Lead paint disclosure is becoming less a problem, largely because it has been outlawed since the late 1970s, but also because by now older homes have been purged of the contaminant. That is no guarantee that your home was one, and while lead paint may not be a problem to you in your ancestral home, the incoming buyer may have children and children have been known to ingest the lead. By now, the Federal (US) and Commonwealth (Canada) jurisdictions have established legal requirements. If the seller doesn't comply, he or she can be sued.

The Fault Lies—in the ground, supposedly. Wherever there is a natural hazard, buyers must be warned. Earthquake faults, tornado occurrence, floodplains, wildfire exposure can all be things that pose a financial risk to the buyer. He may know, but the issue isn't to decide what he will do because of them but for him to decide what risk he is willing to accept and therefore to acquire insurance protection for that risk.

A property that has a history, either negative or positive, should be disclosed. Some jurisdictions are stringent about informing buyers of where murders have taken place, where people with diseases have resided, where reputations of aberrant behavior are lodged. Often, because of the property's historical importance—or proximity to another property where it exists—there may be limitations on remodeling, changing of property character, or use of the property that conflicts with where the property is located.

In its quest for the removal of misleading information, there is a natural worry that disclosure will abort the sale. It's possible, of course. It's also possible that the property's position near a historical landmark will enhance the sale. Otherwise, there is the availability of another bargaining chip. That's not all bad. You might be willing to exchange a small piece of the asking price for the removal of a specific but disclosed piece of information. You're not required to fix all things that are disclosed, assuming you are capable of doing so. There is a price to pay for ignoring them.

Title Insurance

You have a home with a price tag that may reach well into six figures. That property has changed hand, perhaps, several times since being built. Who know what changes the property has undergone since it was built?

The homeowner needs title insurance. It is an errors-and-omissions policy against people mistakes and undiscovered issues made as the paperwork for your property has been handled. How it is obtained and who pays for it is subject to local custom, but it is something that must be done only once.

It's an old joke, but it has been claimed that some original property records were recorded on birch bark. To someone seeking clear title to a property, it may seem that way. Over the years, the information was recorded in property journals, heavy books filed in dusty vaults and written in a hundred different and often indecipherable handwriting styles. We are blessed nowadays that those records are now computerized.

There are public records of such things as ownership, transfer, taxed, liens—municipal and private—and many other facets applying to your property.

A title search is a backward search along the chain of title, beginning with the most recent deed and moving backward as the property changes hands and the deed is rewritten. Assuming the chain of title is intact, eventually the search will uncover the first owner of record, often referred to as the "grantor." Theoretically, the property was identified as a function of the legal jurisdiction, the first grantor. It then was passed from grantor to grantee, hand over hand, until today. If the chain has been broken, or encumbrances have been placed on it, the title search will "heal" the property by documenting the break and ensuring that encumbrances have been properly discharged. Titles have also been affected by easements placed on the property to entitle access to the land for roads, utility cables or lines, for example. Easements are often instituted for people with landlocked property, where access must be obtained to cross the adjacent property. Rights of Way and Easements are important—a property owner cannot build in that area.

A property may be subject to covenants, conditions, and restrictions. These are rules imposed on the deed by a builder, a developer, a neighborhood association, or for gated communities, condos, townhomes, or planned developments. Some are meaningful; some are trivial; some are of downright nuisance value. Age restrictions apply here, as do parking regulation (e.g., alternative side of road parking), limitations as to what can be left outside the house (e.g., how many "junk" cars can be on the property). Some older discrimination-based restrictions are no longer legal, but may simply be ignored.

Registrars sometimes must go beyond the property documents and search marriage and death records and tax sale documents to put together an accurate picture of the history of the home.

There may be many variations, but three types of title insurance are most often available: Basic Owner's, Basic Lenders, and Extended Coverage:

The Basic Owner's Title Policy provides clear title to the property, protection if the documents have been incorrectly signed, protection from forgery and fraud, protection for defective recording, and the identification of restrictive covenants, encumbrances, and judgments. The Basic Lender's Title Policy covers mechanic's liens, liens that have yet to be recorded, unrecorded easements and access rights, and protects against defects and other unrecorded documents. The extended coverage will also insure against building permit and covenant violations from previous owners, structural damage from mineral extractions, and protection against encroachments and forgeries after the issuance of title insurance.

The Home Warranty

One of the things you as the FSBO seller can do for your buyer is to buy a home warranty policy. It's not expensive but it will keep old ghosts from haunting you. Nothing mandates that you do this. In fact, as the deed changes name, the buyer will hear from warranty agencies.

The idea of a home warranty is to provide funds to fix anything in the home that fails and to do so affordably. It's not a safety net, and it's not homeowner's insurance. Homeowner's insurance will provide coverage for files, hail, property crimes, water and wind damage, and several other items involving the homeowner's personal possessions. No, a home warranty covers specific components of the home. It is a contract between a homeowner and a home warranty company that provides discounted repair or replacement services on the home's major systems—furnace, air-conditioning, plumbing, and electrical. It may also cover ranges, refrigerators, washers, and dryers conveyed with the home.

When something happens, home warranty companies will arrange repair or replacement with someone on a list of approved providers. The homeowner pays a small service fee for each service, plus the annual premium cost of the policy. The catch, if there is one, is that different repair/replacement needs involve different service contractors and therefore different service fees once a call has been made.

Home warranty policies are written for basic coverage, but they are not always written for the full replacement cost of the defective item, nor will everything in the home be automatically covered. Those who want additional coverage must arrange for it above the cost of the basic coverage.

The idea of a home warranty is to protect against expensive, unforeseen repair bills. For a buyer who has spent his cash, this may be a very wise decision, particularly if the new homeowner isn't handy, doesn't wish to become his own general contractor, or simply couldn't afford to replace an expensive refrigerator. It's also important to mention that a home warranty is not a substitute for a complete and accurate inspection.

A home warranty is a leveler. The buyer has no idea how any major appliance has been maintained or, for that matter, what surprises lie within the walls. If you, the FSBO seller, were to offer to pay for the first year of a home warranty, might it sway the buyer to your point of view?

Not everything in a home warranty is roses. Just as the buyer hasn't a clue how something has been maintained, it's possible that the repair contractor doesn't know either—or worse, knows too well that the maintenance hasn't been done. Home warranties are written with exclusions for lack of maintenance and evidence of abuse. Because many major appliances are now very pricey, there may be limits to what the policy is willing to cover. Further, the policy might replace an appliance with a bottom-of-the-line model and not permit that charge to be applied to something better. In addition, your choice of repair contractors is limited to the list maintained by the agency that offers the warranty.

Home warranties are often denied where it can be proved there had been improper maintenance, unusual wear and tear, improper installation, or code violations. It also will not cover sprinkler systems, faucet repairs, permit fees, haul-aways, and pools—though it is possible to add to the policy for them. Not all policies pay to repair garage door openers, washers, and dryers.

The kind of things it will cover include air-conditioning, dishwashers, doorbells, furnace / heating, water heater, ductwork, the garbage disposal, inside plumbing stoppages, ceiling fans, electrical systems, range and oven, and communications wiring.

One of the advantages of dealing with an agent who assists FSBO sellers is that she will know the reputable home warranty company that will pay for legitimate repairs when they are needed.

Home warranties differ according to where you are located. The result for both the seller and the buyer can be expressed as POMG—Peace of Mind Guaranteed.

The Walk-through

It's too late to negotiate now, but it's not too late for the buyer to ensure that what he thought he was getting, he was, in fact, receiving. Therefore, as the FSBO seller, though you have lived there for twenty years, it's time for you to operate as if you were the buyer making that final walk-through.

Ideally, you are moved out of the house. You expect the walk-through to happen tomorrow. So today, check what will be tested tomorrow. Exercise the lamps and overhead light switches—all of them. Ensure that all light sockets have burning bulbs in them.

Walk around the house, flush the toilets, open the showers, and turn on the faucets. Let them run for a few moments, and then turn them off. Now check for leaks.

Test every appliance staying with the house. All the burners and ovens on the range should be checked. Open and shut the doors of refrigerators and freezers and where necessary, ensure that the 15-watt light bulb is working.

Test the garage door opener—open and close it. Interrupt its flow and then close it.

Open and close all doors—both interior and exterior.

Take time to peruse the ceilings, check the floors, and scan the walls.

Run all exhaust fans, turn the garbage disposal on and off, kick the heat on and off; do the same to the air-conditioning.

Open and close all windows and storms, if installed. Combination and tilt-in windows should be individually tested.

Finally, clear away any remaining debris.

Ensure that you've filed a change of address with the post office and notified the utilities of a forwarding address for final bills.

Now you're ready. Tomorrow you'll hand over the keys, shake hands with the buyer, climb into your vehicle, and head for your next real estate adventure.